FIRST PERSON

FIRST PERSON:
AN ASTONISHINGLY
FRANK SELF-PORTRAIT
BY RUSSIA'S PRESIDENT
VLADIMIR PUTIN

with Nataliya Gevorkyan, Natalya
Timakova, and Andrei Kolesnikov

Translated by Catherine A. Fitzpatrick

PUBLICAFFAIRS
New York

Contents

Preface

We talked with Vladimir Putin on six separate occasions, for about four hours at a time. Both he and we were patient and tolerant; he, when we asked uncomfortable questions or were too invasive; we, when he was late or asked us to turn the tape recorder off. "That's very personal," he would say.

These were meetings "with our jackets off," although we all still wore ties. Usually they happened late at night. And we only went to his office in the Kremlin once.

Why did we do this? Essentially, we wanted to answer the same question that Trudy Rubin of the *Philadelphia Inquirer* asked in Davos in January: "Who is Putin?" Rubin's question had been addressed to a gathering of prominent Russian politicians and businessmen. And instead of an answer, there was a pause.

We felt that the pause dragged on too long. And it was a legitimate question. Who was this Mr. Putin?

We talked to Putin about his life. We talked—as people often do in Russia—around the dinner table. Sometimes he arrived exhausted, with drooping eyelids, but he never broke off the conversation. Only once, when it was well past midnight, did he ask politely, "Well then, have you run out of questions, or shall we chat some more?"

Sometimes Putin would pause a while to think about a question, but he would always answer it eventually. For example, when we asked whether he had ever been betrayed, he was silent a long time. Finally, he decided to say "no," but then added by way of clarification, "My friends didn't betray me."

We sought out Putin's friends, people who know him well or who have played an important role in his destiny. We went out to his dacha, where we found a bevy of women: his wife, Lyudmila, two daughters–Masha and Katya–and a poodle with a hint of the toy dog in her, named Toska.

We have not added a single editorial line in the book. It holds only our questions. And if those questions led Putin or his relatives to reminisce or ponder, we tried not to interrupt. That's why the book's format is a bit unusual–it consists entirely of interviews and monologues.

All of our conversations are recorded in these pages. They might not answer the complex question of "Who is this Mr. Putin?," but at least they will bring us a little bit closer to understanding Russia's newest president.

NATALIYA GEVORKYAN
NATALYA TIMAKOVA
ANDREI KOLESNIKOV

Principle Figures
in First Person

People

VADIM VIKTOROVICH BAKATIN:
USSR interior minister (1988–90); chairman of KGB (1991); presidential candidate.

BORIS ABRAMOVICH BEREZOVSKY:
Prominent businessman influential in political affairs; part-owner of ORT, pro-government public television station; former deputy secretary of Security Council, October 1996–November 1997; involved in the Chechen conflict; appointed executive secretary of the Commonwealth of Independent States (CIS); dismissed by Yeltsin in March 1999, elected member of parliament from Karachaevo-Cherkessia in December 1999.

PAVEL PAVLOVICH BORODIN:
Chief of staff in the presidential administration from 1993 to 2000; In January 2000, appointed state secretary of the Union of Belarus and Russia.

LEONID ILYICH BREZHNEV:
General secretary of the Communist Party of the Soviet Union from 1964–1982.

ANATOLY BORISOVICH CHUBAIS:
Vice premier in the Chernomyrdin government (1992) and government (1994); appointed member of the government commission handling privatization and structural adjustment in 1993; appointed first deputy chair of the government in 1994 and dismissed by Yeltsin in January 1996; appointed by Yeltsin to post of chief of presidential administration in July 1996; Minister of Finance, March–November 1997.

VLADIMIR CHUROV:
Deputy chair of the Committee for Foreign Liason of the St. Petersburg Mayor's Office in Sobchak administration.

MICHAEL FROLOV:
Retired colonel, Putin's instructor at the Andropov Red Banner Institute.

VERA DMITRIEVNA GUREVICH:
Putin's schoolteacher from grades 4 to 8 in School No. 193 in St. Petersburg.

SERGEI BORISOVICH IVANOV:
Foreign intelligence career officer with rank of lieutenant general; appointed deputy director of FSB in August 1998; appointed secretary of the Security Council in November 1999.

KATYA:
Putin's younger daughter.

SERGEI VLADILENOVICH KIRIENKO:
First deputy minister of energy in 1997; appointed chair of the government (prime minister) in April 1998 and dismissed by Yeltsin in August 1998, elected member of parliament from the party list of the Union of Right Forces.

ALEKSANDR VASILYEVICH KORZHAKOV:
Hired as Boris Yeltsin's bodyguard in 1985 when Yeltsin was first secretary of the Moscow City Party Committee and continued to

manage Yeltsin's security in subsequent positions; awarded the rank of general in 1992; joined the Yeltsin election campaign in 1996 and was dismissed from all his posts in June 1996 after disagreements about how to run the campaign.

VLADIMIR ALEKSANDROVICH KRYUCHKOV:
Chairman of the Soviet KGB (1988–91) until arrested for the August 1991 coup; amnestied in February 1994.

YURI LUZHKOV:
Mayor of Moscow.

MASHA:
Putin's older daughter.

YEVGENY MAKSIMOVICH PRIMAKOV:
Pravda columnist and former director of the USSR Institute of Oriental Studies and the Institute of World Economy and International Relations, first deputy chairman of the KGB (1991), director of the Soviet Central Intelligence Service (1991), and then director of the Russian Foreign Intelligence Service (1991–1996); appointed Foreign Minister January 1996 and again in 1998; appointed by Yeltsin's decree to the position of chair of the government (prime minister) in September 1998 and dismissed by Yeltsin from this position in May 1999; elected to the State Duma (parliament) from the party list of Fatherland–All Russia in December 1999.

LYUDMILA PUTINA:
Vladimir Putin's wife (nicknames found in text: Luda, Ludik).

SERGEI ROLDUGIN:
Lead cellist in the Mariinsky Theater Symphony Orchestra, a friend of the Putins, and godfather of Putin's older daughter, Masha.

EDUARD AMVROSIEVICH SHEVARDNADZE:
Soviet foreign minister (1985–91) who resigned in protest of the impending coup; co-chairman of Democratic Reform Movement (1991–92); head of state and chairman of parliament of Georgia.

ANATOLY ALEKSANDROVICH SOBCHAK:
Mayor and chair of the government of St. Petersburg (Leningrad)
from 1991 to 1996; co-chairman of Democratic Reform Movement (1991–92); member of the Russian Presidential Council since
1992; died in February 2000. His wife is Lyudmila Borisnova.

OLEG NIKOLAYEVICH SOSKOVETS:
Appointed first deputy chair of the government in 1993 (deputy
prime minister) responsible for 14 ministries, including energy and
transportation; assigned to deal with the Chechen conflict in 1994;
joined Yeltsin presidential campaign team in 1996 but dismissed in
March from the campaign, and, in June, was relieved of his post as
first vice premier.

YURI SKURATOV:
Former Prosecutor General, suspended after a newspaper published a photograph of him in a steam bath with two prostitutes.

VLADIMIR ANATOLYEVICH YAKOVLEV:
First deputy mayor of St. Petersburg from 1993–1996; elected governor of St. Petersburg in 1996.

MARINA YENTALTSEVA:
Putin's secretary at the St. Petersburg City Council (1991–96).

VALENTIN YUMASHEV:
Chief of staff in the Yeltsin administration

Terms

FRG	Federal Republic of Germany
FSB	Federal Security Service
FSK	Federal Counterintelligence Service
FSO	Federal Guard Servic

GDR	German Democratic Republic (East Germany)
KGB	Committee for State Security (Soviet era)
Komsomol	Young Communist League
Kukly	Puppets, a satirical TV show
MVD	Ministry of Internal Affairs or Interior Ministry
NATO	North Atlantic Treaty Organization
NKVD	People's Commissariat for Internal Affairs, or the Stalin-era secret police
OSCE	Organization for Security and Cooperation in Europe, 54-member security and human rights body founded in 1975.
Pioneers	Soviet-era children's organization
SED	East German Communist Party

"In fact, I have had a very simple life. Everything is an open book.

I finished school and went to university.

I graduated from university and went to the KGB.

I finished the KGB and went back to university.

After university, I went to work for Sobchak.

From Sobchak, to Moscow and to the General Department.

Then to the Presidential Administration.

From there, to the FSB.

Then I was appointed Prime Minister.

Now I'm Acting President. That's it!"

"But surely there are more details?"

"Yes, there are. . . ."

Part 1

THE SON

Putin talks about his parents, touching on his father's World War II sabotage missions, the Siege of Leningrad, and life in a communal flat after the war. It isn't easy—no hot water, no bathroom, a stinking toilet, and constant bickering. Putin spends much of his time chasing rats with a stick in the stairwell.

I know more about my father's family than about my mother's. My father's father was born in St. Petersburg and worked as a cook. They were a very ordinary family. A cook, after all, is a cook. But apparently my grandfather cooked rather well, because after World War I he was offered a job in The Hills district on the outskirts of Moscow, where Lenin and the whole Ulyanov family lived. When Lenin died, my grandfather was transferred to one of Stalin's dachas. He worked there a long time.

He wasn't a victim of the purges?

No, for some reason they let him be. Few people who spent much time around Stalin came through unscathed, but my grandfather was one of them. He outlived Stalin, by the way, and in his later, retirement years he was a cook at the Moscow City Party Committee sanitorium in Ilinskoye.

Did your parents talk much about your grandfather?

I have a clear recollection of Ilinskoye myself, because I used to come for visits. My grandfather kept pretty quiet about his past life. My parents didn't talk much about the past, either. People generally didn't, back then. But when relatives would come to visit, there would be long chats around the table, and I would catch some snatches, some fragments of the conversation. But my parents never told me anything about themselves. Especially my father. He was a silent man.

I know my father was born in St. Petersburg in 1911. After World War I broke out, life was hard in the city. People were starving. The whole family moved to my grandmother's home in the village of Pominovo, in the Tver region. Her house is still standing today, by the way; members of the family still spend their vacations there. It was in Pominovo that my father met my mother. They were both 17 years old when they got married.

Why? Did they have a reason to?

No, apparently not. Do you need a reason to get married? The main reason was love. And my father was headed for the army soon. Maybe they each wanted some sort of guarantee. . . . I don't know.

Vera Dmitrievna Gurevich (Vladimir Putin's schoolteacher from grades 4 through 8 in School No. 193):

Volodya's* parents had a very difficult life. Can you imagine how courageous his mother must have been to give birth at age 41? Volodya's father once said to me, "One of our sons would have been your age." I assumed they must have lost another child during the war, but didn't feel comfortable asking about it.

In 1932, Putin's parents came to Peter [St. Petersburg]. They lived in the suburbs, in Peterhof. His mother went to work in a factory and his father was almost immediately drafted into the army, where he served on a submarine fleet. Within a year after he returned, they had two sons. One died a few months after birth.

*Russians use various diminutives for names, depending on degrees of familiarity and affection. Vladimir Putin is often called Vovka and Volodya by his friends and family.

Apparently, when the war broke out, your father went immediately to the front. He was a submariner who had just completed his term of service . . .

Yes, he went to the front as a volunteer.

And your mama?

Mama categorically refused to go anywhere. She stayed at home in Peterhof. When it became extremely hard to go on there, her brother in Peter took her in. He was a naval officer serving at the fleet's headquarters in Smolny.* He came for her and the baby and got them out under gunfire and bombs.

And what about your grandfather, the cook? Didn't he do anything to help them?

No. Back then, people generally didn't ask for favors. I think that under the circumstances it would have been impossible, anyway. My grandfather had a lot of children, and all of his sons were at the front.

So your mother and brother were taken from Peterhof, which was under blockade, to Leningrad, which was also blockaded?

Where else could they go? Mama said that some sort of shelters were being set up in Leningrad, in an effort to save the children's lives. It was in one of those children's homes that my second brother came down with diphtheria and died.

How did she survive?

My uncle helped her. He would feed her out of his own rations. There was a time when he was transferred some-

*Smolny was a private girls' school before the Revolution, when Lenin took it over and made it the headquarters of his revolutionary government. Since then it has been the seat of local government in St. Petersburg.

where for a while, and she was on the verge of starvation. This is no exaggeration. Once my mother fainted from hunger. People thought she had died, and they laid her out with the corpses. Luckily Mama woke up in time and started moaning. By some miracle, she lived. She made it through the entire blockade of Leningrad. They didn't get her out until the danger was past.

And where was your father?

My father was in the battlefield the whole time. He had been assigned to a demolitions battalion of the NKVD. These battalions were engaged in sabotage behind German lines. My father took part in one such operation. There were 28 people in his group. They were dropped into Kingisepp. They took a good look around, set up a position in the forest, and even managed to blow up a munitions depot before they ran out of food. They came across some local residents, Estonians, who brought them food but later gave them up to the Germans.

They had almost no chance of surviving. The Germans had them surrounded on all sides, and only a few people, including my father, managed to break out. Then the chase was on. The remnants of the unit headed off toward the front line. They lost a few more people along the road and decided to split up. My father jumped into a swamp over his head and breathed through a hollow reed until the dogs had passed by. That's how he survived. Only 4 of the 28 men in his unit made it back home.

Then he found your mother? They were reunited?

No, he didn't get a chance to look for her. They sent him right back into combat. He wound up in another tight spot, the so-called Neva Nickel. This was a small, circular area. If you stand with your back to Lake Ladoga, it's on the left bank of the Neva River. The German troops had seized everything except for this small plot of land. And our guys held that spot through the entire blockade, calculating that it would play a role in the final breakthrough. The Germans kept trying to capture it. A fantastic number of bombs were dropped on every square meter of that bit of turf—even by the standards of that war. It was a monstrous massacre. But to be sure, the Neva Nickel played an important role in the end.

Don't you think that we paid too high a price for that little piece of land?

I think that there are always a lot of mistakes made in war. That's inevitable. But when you are fighting, if you keep thinking that everybody around you is always making mistakes, you'll never win. You have to take a pragmatic attitude. And you have to keep thinking of victory. And they were thinking of victory then.

My father was severely wounded in the "Nickel." Once he and another soldier were ordered to capture a prisoner who might talk during interrogation. They crawled up to a foxhole and were just settling in to wait, when suddenly a German came out. The German was surprised, and so were they. The German recovered first, took a grenade out of his pocket, threw it at my father and the other soldier, and calmly went on his way. Life is such a simple little thing, really.

How do you know all this? You said your parents didn't like to talk about themselves.

This is a story that my father told me. The German was probably convinced that he had killed the Russians. But my father survived, although his legs were shot through with shrapnel. Our soldiers dragged him out of there several hours later.

Across the front line?

You guessed it. The nearest hospital was in the city, and in order to get there, they had to drag him all the way across the Neva.

Everyone knew that this would be suicide, because every centimeter of that territory was being shot up. No commander would have issued such an order, of course. And nobody was volunteering. My father had already lost so much blood that it was clear he was going to die soon if they left him there.

Coincidentally, a soldier who happened to be an old neighbor from back home came across him. Without a word, he sized up the situation, hauled my father up onto his back, and carried him across the frozen Neva to the other side. They made an ideal target, and yet they survived. This neighbor dragged my father to the hospital, said goodbye, and went back to the front line. The fellow told my father that they wouldn't see each other again. Evidently he didn't believe he would survive in the "Nickel" and thought that my father didn't have much of a chance either.

Was he wrong?

Thank God, he was. My father managed to survive. He spent several months in the hospital. My mother found him there. She came to see him every day.

Mama herself was half dead. My father saw the shape she was in and began to give her his own food, hiding it from the nurses. To be sure, they caught on pretty quickly and put a stop to it. The doctors noticed that he was fainting from hunger. When they figured out why, they gave him a stern lecture and wouldn't let Mama in to see him for awhile. The upshot was that they both survived. Only my father's injuries left him with a lifelong limp.

And the neighbor?
The neighbor survived, too! After the blockade, he moved to another city. He and my father once met by chance in Leningrad twenty years later. Can you imagine?

Vera Dmitrievna Gurevich:
Volodya's mother was a very nice person—kind, selfless, the soul of goodness. She was not a very educated woman. I don't know if she finished even five grades of school. She worked hard her whole life. She was a janitor, took deliveries in a bakery at night, and washed test tubes in a laboratory. I think she even worked as a guard at a store at one time.

Volodya's papa worked as a toolmaker in a factory. He was much liked and appreciated as a ready and willing worker. For a long time, incidentally, he didn't collect disability, although one of his legs was really crippled. He was the one who usually cooked at home. He used to make a wonderful aspic. We remember that Putin aspic to this day. Nobody could make aspic like he did.

After the war my father was demobilized and went to work as a skilled laborer at the Yegorov Train Car Factory. There is a little plaque in each metro car that says, "This is car number such-and-such, manufactured at the Yegorov Train Car Factory."

The factory gave Papa a room in a communal apartment in a typical St. Petersburg building on Baskov Lane, in the center of town. It had an inner airshaft for a courtyard, and my parents lived on the fifth floor. There was no elevator.

Before the war, my parents had half of a house in Peterhof. They were very proud of their standard of living then. So this was a step down.

Vera Dmitrievna Gurevich:

They had a horrid apartment. It was communal, without any conveniences. There was no hot water, no bathtub. The toilet was horrendous. It ran smack up against a stair landing. And it was so cold—just awful—and the stairway had a freezing metal handrail. The stairs weren't safe either—there were gaps everywhere.

There, on that stair landing, I got a quick and lasting lesson in the meaning of the word *cornered*. There were hordes of rats in the front entryway. My friends and I used to chase them around with sticks. Once I spotted a huge rat and pursued it down the hall until I drove it into a corner. It had nowhere to run. Suddenly it lashed around and threw itself at me. I was surprised and frightened. Now the rat was chasing me. It jumped across the landing and down the stairs. Luckily, I was a little faster and I managed to slam the door shut in its nose.

Vera Dmitrievna Gurevich:

There was practically no kitchen. It was just a square, dark hallway without windows. A gas burner stood on one side and a sink on the other. There was no room to move around.

Behind this so-called kitchen lived the neighbors, a family of three. And other neighbors, a middle-aged couple, were next door. The apartment was communal. And the Putins were squeezed into one room. By the standards of those days it was decent, though, because it measured about 20 meters square.

A Jewish family—an elderly couple and their daughter, Hava—lived in our communal apartment. Hava was a grown woman, but as the adults used to say, her life hadn't turned out well. She had never married, and she still lived with her parents.

Her father was a tailor, and although he seemed quite elderly, he would stitch on his sewing machine for whole days at a time. They were religious Jews. They did not work on the Sabbath, and the old man would recite the Talmud, droning away. Once, I couldn't hold back any longer and asked what he was chanting. He explained about the Talmud, and I immediately lost interest.

As is usually the case in a communal apartment, people clashed now and then. I always wanted to defend my parents, and speak up on their behalf. I should explain here that I got along very well with the elderly couple, and often played on their side of the apartment. Well, one day, when they were having words with my parents, I jumped in. My parents were furious. Their reaction came as a complete shock to me; it was incomprehensible. I was sticking up for them, and they shot back with, "Mind your own business!" Why? I just couldn't understand it. Later, I realized that my parents considered my good rapport with the old couple, and the couple's affection for me, much more important than those petty kitchen spats. After that incident, I never got involved in the kitchen quarrels again. As soon as they started fighting, I simply went back into our room, or over to the old folks' room. It didn't matter to me which.

There were other pensioners living in our apartment as well, although they weren't there long. They played a role in my baptism. Baba Anya was a religious person, and she used to go to church. When I was born, she and my mother had me baptized. They kept it a secret from my father, who was a party member and secretary of the party organization in his factory shop.

Many years later, in 1993, when I worked on the Leningrad City Council, I went to Israel as part of an official delegation. Mama gave me my baptismal cross to get it blessed at the Lord's Tomb. I did as she said and then put the cross around my neck. I have never taken it off since.

Part 2

THE SCHOOLBOY

Interviews with Putin's schoolteacher reveal a bad student with a bright mind. Putin is always late for school and doesn't make it into the Pioneers. But then, at age 10, he discovers the martial arts and, after reading novels and watching spy movies, develops a single-minded ambition to join the KGB. At 16 he troops over to the KGB headquarters where he's told that he has to go to law school and keep his mouth shut if he really wants to be a spy. Despite the pleas and threats of his parents and judo coaches, he decides to do just that.

Do you remember first grade?

I was born in October, so I did not start school until I was almost eight years old. We still have the photo in our family archive: I am in an old-fashioned, gray school uniform. It looks like a military uniform, and for some reason I'm standing with a flowerpot in my hand. Not a bouquet, but a pot.

Did you want to go to school?

No, not especially. I liked playing outside, in our courtyard. There were two courtyards joined together, like an airshaft, and my whole life took place there. Mama sometimes stuck her head out the window and shouted "Are you in the courtyard?" I always was. As long as I didn't run away, I was allowed to go play in the courtyard without asking for permission.

And you never once disobeyed?

When I was five or six, I walked out to the corner of the big street without permission. It was on the First of May. I looked around me. People were rushing around and making a lot of noise. The street was very busy. I was even a little afraid.

Then one winter, when I was a little bit older, my friends

and I decided to leave the city without telling our parents. We wanted to go on a trip. We got off the train somewhere and were completely lost. It was cold. We had brought some matches and somehow managed to start a fire. We had nothing to eat. We froze completely. Then we got back on the train and headed home. We got the belt for that stunt. And we never wanted to go on another trip again.

So you stopped looking for adventures?

For a time. Especially when I went to school. From first through eighth grade, I went to School No. 193, which was in the same lane as my house, about a seven-minute walk. I was always late for my first class, so even in the winter, I didn't dress very warmly. It took up a lot of time to get dressed, run to school, and then take off my coat. So in order to save time, I never put on a coat, and just shot out to school like a bullet and got right behind my desk.

Did you like school?

For a time. As long as I managed to be—what would you call it?—the unspoken leader. The school was right next door to my house. Our courtyard was a reliable refuge, and that helped.

Did people listen to you?

I didn't try to command people. It was more important to preserve my independence. If I had to compare it with my adult life, I would say that the role I played as a kid was like the role of the judicial branch, and not the executive. And as long as I managed to do that, I liked school.

But it didn't last. It soon became clear that my courtyard skills were not enough, and I began to play sports. And in order to maintain my social status I had to start doing well in school. Up until the sixth grade, to be honest, I had been a pretty haphazard student.

Vera Dmitrievna Gurevich:

I met Volodya when he was still in the fourth grade. His teacher, Tamara Pavlovna Chizhova, once said to me, "Vera Dmitrievna, take my class. The kids aren't bad."

I went to visit the class and organized a German language club. It was interesting to see who showed up. About 10–12 students came. Tamara Pavlovna asked me who was there. I told her: Natasha Soldatova, Volodya Putin . . . She was surprised. "Volodya, too? That doesn't seem like him." But he showed great interest in the lessons.

She said, "Well, just you wait. He'll show you." "What do you mean?" I asked. She replied that he was too sneaky and disorganized. He wasn't even in the Pioneers. Usually you are accepted into the Pioneers in the third grade. But Volodya wasn't because he was such a cutup.

Some classes studied English, and others German. English was more in fashion than German, and there were more English classes. Volodya ended up in my class. In fifth grade, he hadn't really proven himself, but I sensed that he had potential, energy, and character. I saw his great interest in the language. He picked it up easily. He had a very good memory, a quick mind.

I thought: This kid will make something of himself. I decided to devote more attention to him and discourage him from hanging out with the boys on the street. He had friends from the neighborhood, two brothers by the name of Kovshov, and he used to prowl around with them, jumping from the roofs of the garages and sheds. Volodya's father didn't like that very much. His papa had very strict morals. But we couldn't get Volodya away from those Kovshov brothers.

His father was very serious and imposing. He often had an angry look. The first time I came to see him, I was even frightened. I thought, "What a strict man." And then it turned out that he was very kindhearted. But there were no kisses. There was none of that lovey-dovey stuff in their house.

Once when I came to visit, I said to Volodya's father, "Your son is not work-ing to his full potential." And he said, "Well, what can I do? Kill him, or what?" And I said, "You have to have a talk with him. Let's work on him together, you at home, and I at school. He could be getting better than C's. He catches everything on the fly." At any rate, we agreed to work on him; but in the end, we had no particular influence.

Volodya himself changed very abruptly in the sixth grade. It was obvious; he had set himself a goal. Most likely he had understood that he had to achieve something in life. He began to get better grades, and did it easily.

Finally, he was accepted into the Pioneers. There was a ceremony and we went on a trip to Lenin's home, where he was inducted into the Pioneers. Right after that he became chair of his unit's council.

Why weren't you taken into the Pioneers until the sixth grade? Was everything really so bad up until then?

Of course. I was a hooligan, not a Pioneer.

Are you being coy?

You insult me. I really was a bad boy.

Vera Dmitrievna Gurevich:

Most of the kids liked to go to dances. We had evening events at the school. We called it the Crystal Club. And we put on plays. But Volodya didn't take part in any of this. His father really wanted him to play the accordion and forced him to take lessons in the early grades. Volodya resisted it. Although he did love to pluck away on the guitar. He sang mainly Vysotsky,* all of the songs from the album *Vertical*, about the stars, and about Seryozha from Malaya Bronnaya Street.

But he didn't like socializing much. He preferred sports. He started doing martial arts in order to learn how to defend himself. Four times a week he took

---

Vladimir Vysotsky was a popular Russian folksinger.

classes somewhere near the Finland Station, and he got pretty good. He loved his sambo. And then he started taking part in competitions, which often required him to travel to other cities.

I got into sports when I was about 10 or 11. As soon as it became clear that my pugnacious nature was not going to keep me king of the courtyard or schoolgrounds, I decided to go into boxing. But I didn't last long there. I quickly got my nose broken. The pain was terrible. I couldn't even touch the tip of my nose. But even though everyone was telling me I needed an operation, I didn't go to the doctor. Why? I knew it would heal by itself. And it did. But I lost my boxing bug after that.

Then I decided to go in for sambo, a Soviet combination of judo and wrestling. Martial arts were popular at the time. I went to a class near my house and began to work out. It was a very plain gym that belonged to the Trud athletic club. I had a very good trainer there, Anatoly Semyonovich Rakhlin. He devoted his whole life to his art, and is still training girls and boys to this day.

Anatoly Semyonovich played a decisive role in my life. If I hadn't gotten involved in sports, I'm not sure how my life would have turned out. It was sports that dragged me off the streets. To be honest, the courtyard wasn't a very good environment for a kid.

At first I studied sambo. Then judo. Coach decided that we would all switch to judo, and we did.

Judo is not just a sport, you know. It's a philosophy. It's respect for your elders and for your opponent. It's not for weaklings. Everything in judo has an instructive aspect. You come out onto the mat, you bow to one another, you follow ritual. It could be done differently, you know. Instead of bowing to your opponent, you could jab him in the forehead.

Did you ever smoke?

No. I tried it a couple of times, but I never smoked regularly. And when I began to do sports, I simply ruled it out. I used to work out every other day, and then every day. Soon I had no time left for anything else. I had other priorities; I had to prove myself in sports, achieve something. I set goals. Sports really had a strong influence on me.

And you didn't try karate? That was popular in those days, even thought it was banned.

We thought karate and all other noncontact sports were like ballet. Sports was only sports if you had to shed sweat and blood and work hard.

Even when karate became popular and karate schools of all sorts began springing up, we viewed them purely as moneymaking enterprises. We, on the other hand, never paid any money for our lessons. We all came from poor families. And since karate lessons cost money from the start, the kids taking karate thought they were first class.

Once we went to the gym with Leonid Ionovich, the senior coach from Trud. The karate students were working out on the mat, although it was our turn. Leonid went up to their trainer and told him it was time for our class. The karate trainer didn't even look his way—as if to say, get lost. Then Leonid, without saying a word, flipped him, squeezed him lightly, and dragged him off the mat. He had lost consciousness. Then Leonid turned to us and said, "Go on in and take your places." That was our attitude toward karate.

Did your parents encourage you to take these lessons?

No, just the opposite. At first, they were very suspicious. They thought I was acquiring some sort of ugly skill to use on the street. Later, when they met the trainer and he began to visit our home, their attitude changed. And when I achieved my first successes, my parents understood that judo was a serious and useful art.

You started winning?
Yes, within about a year or two.

Vera Dmitrievna Gurevich:
I taught Volodya from fifth through eighth grade. And then we had to decide what school to send him to. Most of the class went to School No. 197 on Petra Lavrova Street. But Volodya and Slava Yakovlev chose a school with a special focus on chemistry. I think Slava talked him into it.

I was surprised at the time. But Volodya told me, "We'll study there a while, and then we'll see." He was never hasty. He also got good grades in that school. He had a wonderful teacher named Minna Moiseyevna Yuditskaya. She also taught German. And oddly, I visited the Putins' home even more often than I had before, as I was helping Volodya with his German. I wanted him to speak German well. He would help me too. Besides teaching elementary school, I taught in the evenings at a technical school for architects and builders. Once, my husband had to go away on a business trip. My daughters were still little at the time. So I said, "Volodya, help me out. I'm coming home late and my girls might be afraid if they wake up." He would come and look in on them and even stay the night.

I think Volodya is a good person. But he never forgives people who betray him or are mean to him. In any case, that's what I think.

Volodya wasn't very popular in his new school, as far as I could tell. But he did have a literature class with a teacher named Kochergin who made the lessons really creative and interesting. I remember one of the topics quite well that he assigned for student compositions. It was unusual for those times: "A revolution has a beginning, a revolution has no end." Well, you could write a whole treatise on that one!

Right after graduating from school, Volodya announced that he was going to law school. I don't know what influenced his choice. Why law school? We had thought originally that he would go to a technical institute. Lena Gryaznova went to the technical institute, and they were close. There was much that linked Volodya and Lena. She had starting coming over to the Putin house as early as sixth grade. Volodya was not especially interested in girls; but they were certainly interested in him.

So all of a sudden, he announced to everyone: "I'm going to university." And I said "How?" And he said "I"ll solve that problem myself."

Even before I graduated from school, I wanted to work in intelligence. It was a dream of mine, although it seemed about as likely as a flight to Mars. And sure, my ambitions sometimes changed. I also wanted to be a sailor. And at one point I really wanted to be a pilot.

The Academy of Civil Aviation is in Leningrad, and I was hell-bent on getting in. I read the literature and even subscribed to an aviation journal. But then books and spy movies like *The Sword and the Shield* took hold of my imagination. What amazed me most of all was how one man's effort could achive what whole armies could not. One spy could decide the fate of thousands of people. At least, that's the way I understood it.

The Academy of Civil Aviation quickly lost its thrill. I had made my choice. I wanted to be a spy.

My parents didn't understand this right away. My coach had gone to see them and told them that as an athlete, I could get into an institute practically without passing exams. So they tried to talk me into going to an institute. My coach took their side. He couldn't understand why I was resisting. "He has a 100 percent chance of getting into that Academy of

Civil Aviation," he told my parents. "And if he doesn't get into university, then he'll have to go into the army."

It was a difficult situation. My father had a very commanding personality. But I dug my heels in and said I had made up my mind.

Then another coach of mine from the Trud Club, Leonid Ionovich, came to visit. He was a clever guy. "Well," he said to me. "Where are you going?" Of course he already knew. He was just acting sly. I said, "To university." "Oh, that's great, good for you," he said, "in what department?" "The law school," I answered. Then he roared: "What?! To catch people? What are you doing? You'll be a cop. Do you understand?!" I was insulted. "I'm not going to be a cop!" I yelled back.

For a year, they put pressure on me every day. That only increased my desire to go to law school. But why law school? Let me explain.

In order to find out how to become a spy, sometime back around the beginning of the ninth grade, I had gone to the office of the KGB Directorate. A guy came out and listened to me. "I want to get a job with you," I said. "That's terrific, but there are several issues," he said. "First, we don't take people who come to us on their own initiative. Second, you can come to us only after the army or after some type of civilian higher education."

I was intrigued. "What kind of higher education?" I asked. "Any!" he said. He probably just wanted to get rid of me. "But what kind is preferred?" I asked. "Law school." And that was that. From that moment on, I began to prepare for the law faculty of Leningrad University. And nobody could stop me.

But my parents and my coaches tried. They threatened me with the prospect of the army for a long time. What they didn't understand was that the army suited me just fine. Of course it would have slowed my progress a little, but it wouldn't deter me from my decision.

The coaches, however, had more tricks up their sleeves. When I went to enroll in preparatory classes at the university, I learned that they had made up lists of athletes who were to be given priority in university admissions. I knew for a fact that I wasn't on any list. But when I was enrolling in classes, my gym teacher tried to force me to join the Burevestnik Club. I asked him, "How come I have to switch over to this?" And he said, "We helped get you into the university, so please be so kind . . ." I knew something was up.

I went to the dean. I walked in and and told him outright, "I'm being forced to transfer into Burevestnik. I don't think I should do that." And the dean, Prof. Alekseyev, a kindhearted, good man, said, "Why are they forcing you?" And I said, "Because they supposedly helped me, as an athlete, to get into the university, and now I must pay them back by joining Burevestnik."

He said, "Really? That can't be! Everyone gets into this university on equal terms, judged according to their knowledge, not by some list of athletes. Wait a minute, and I'll find out." Then he reached into his desk, got a list out, glanced at it, and asked me my last name. "You're not on the list," he said, "So you can safely tell everybody to get lost." Which I did.

Nevertheless, in intervarsity championships I played on behalf of the university team, as I could do this without transferring from one sports club to the other. Still, the coaches didn't let up their efforts to recruit me. I told them a hundred times that I would not leave Trud—all my friends were there, and my first coach. I said I would never join another club. I would play for the one I wanted.

Part 3

THE UNIVERSITY STUDENT

Putin studies hard at the university, but still finds time to cruise Leningrad in his Zaporozhets car and compete in judo tournaments. Over the summer he works in construction with his buddies. He has romances and breakups, but his primary passion remains intact: finding a way into the KGB.

Was it hard to get into university?

Yes, it was, because there were 100 slots and only 10 of them were reserved for high school graduates. The rest were for army guys. So for us high-schoolers, the competition was fierce; something like 40 kids per slot. I had gotten a B in composition but A's in all my other subjects, and I was accepted. By the way, at that time, they didn't take into account the total grade point average of the applicant. So in tenth grade I could completely devote myself to the subjects that I would have to pass to get into university. If I hadn't dropped the other subjects, I wouldn't have gotten in.

Thank God, we had very smart teachers with sharp tactics in our school. Their main goal was to prepare students to get into college. And as soon as they realized that I wasn't going to become a chemist and wanted to major in the humanities, they didn't interfere. In fact, quite the opposite—they approved.

You evidently studied hard in university, with your future in mind?

Yes, I studied hard. I didn't become involved in any extracurricular activities. I wasn't a Komsomol functionary.

Was your stipend enough to cover your living expenses?

No, it wasn't enough. At first, my parents had to support me. I was a student, and didn't have any money. I could have earned extra money working construction like a lot of people. But what would have been the point? I was on a construction crew once. I went to Komi, where I chopped trees for the lumber industry and repaired houses. I finished the job and they handed me a packet of money, probably about 1,000 rubles. In those days, a car cost 3,500 or 4,000 rubles. But for a month and a half of work, we got 1,000! So it was good money. Actually, fantastic money.

We earned our pay. And then we had to spend it on something. My two friends and I went to Gagry on vacation without even stopping back in Leningrad. We got there, and on the first day we got drunk chasing shish kebabs down with port wine. Then we tried to think of what to do next. Where could we go to spend the night? There were probably some hotels around, but we didn't have much hope of getting into them. Late at night, we finally found an old lady who agreed to take us in and give us a room.

We spent several days swimming, tanning, and getting good rest. But soon we had to get out of there and somehow get back home. We were running out of money. We came up with a plan; we would finagle places on the deck of a steamship on its way to Odessa. Then we would take a train to Peter, buying tickets for the top bunks in the sleepers, which were the cheapest.

We pooled our pocket change and realized we had nothing but a few kopecks left for provisions. We decided to buy some *tushonka,* some canned stew, for the trip. One of the fellows was rather careful—he had more money left over than the other, who was a spendthrift. When we told the more economical friend that he should share his dough, he thought for a minute and then said, "That canned meat is pretty hard on the stomach. That's not really the right thing to get." And we said, "Whatever you say. Let's get going."

When we got down to the docks, a huge crowd had gathered. The ship was giant as well—a beautiful white ocean-liner. We were told that only passengers with tickets to the cabins were being allowed on, and those with deck seats were not yet being admitted. All the deck passengers had little tickets made out of hard cardboard, but we had larger-sized, mixed-passage tickets that looked like the ones first-class passengers would have had.

My friend who had refused to chip in for the canned meat said, "You know, I don't like the look of this. I don't think it's going to work out. Let's try to get on right now." I said, "It's awkward, let's just stand here and wait our turn." He said, "Well, you can stand around if you want. We're going to get on." So they went to board the ship, and of course I ran after them.

The ticket-taker asked us what kind of tickets we had. "We have the big ones," we answered. He waved us on.

So we were let on board the ship with the first-class passengers. And then the foreman or somebody else yelled, "Are there any others for first class?" The crowd on the dock was silent.

He asked once again, "Are there only deck passengers left?" The crowd, hoping they would now be allowed on, cried out excitedly, "Yes, just deck passengers!" To which he shouted, "Raise the plank!"

They lifted the walkway, and suddenly panic broke out on the dock. People were furious. They had been deceived. They had paid money, and now they weren't being let on the ship.

Later they were told that there was a freight overage and that the ship was full.

If we hadn't gotten on board when we did, we would have been left standing on the dock. And we didn't have a single kopeck left. I don't know what we would have done.

So we settled into some lifeboats, which hung out over the water. And that was how we got home, as if we were lying in hammocks. For two nights I looked up at the sky, and I couldn't take my eyes away. The ship sailed on, and the stars seemed to just hang there. Do you know what I mean? Sailors may be used to that, but for me it was a wondrous discovery.

That first evening we ogled the cabin passengers. It made us a little wistful to see how wonderful their lives were. All we had were the lifeboats, the stars, and the tins of *tushonka.*

Our thrifty friend didn't have any canned meat. He couldn't hold out any longer, and went to the restaurant. But the prices there were so high that he quickly came back and said indifferently, "Well, I suppose I wouldn't mind scarfing down a little *tushonka.*" But my other friend, who kept strictly to the rules, said, "You know, you should worry about your stomach. It's not good for you." So the thrifty guy starved for a day after that. It was cruel, of course, but it was also fair.

When I went to university, I started concentrating on my studies. Athletics took second place. But I did work out regularly and took part in all the All-Union competitions, although it was just by habit, really.

In 1976, I became the city-wide champion. The people in our section included not only amateurs, like me, but also professionals and European and Olympic champions in both sambo and judo.

I became a sambo master black belt after entering university, and then a judo master two years later. I don't know how it is nowadays, but back then you had to collect a certain number of victories over opponents of a certain level, and to place in serious competitions. For example, you had to be among the top three in the city or get first place in the All-Union competition for Trud.

I remember a couple matches vividly. After one of them I couldn't even breathe, only croak. My opponent was a strong guy, and I had used up so much energy that I just wheezed instead of inhaling and exhaling. I won, but only by a slim margin.

And then there was the time I lost to the world champion, Volodya Kullenin. Later he began to drink heavily and was murdered on the street. But in university he was a fine athlete, really brilliant and talented. He hadn't started drinking when I fought him. We were competing for the city championship. He was already world champion. Right away, during the first minutes, I threw him across my back—and did it gracefully, with ease. In principle, the match should have ended right then, but since Kullenin was world champion, it wouldn't have been right to stop the fight. So they gave me some points and we continued. Of course Kullenin was stronger than me, but I fought hard. Under the rules of this martial art, any sort of crying out is considered a signal of defeat. When Kullenin twisted my elbow backward, the judge seemed to hear me make some grunts. So Kullenin was declared the victor. I remember that match to this day. And I was not ashamed to lose to a world champion.

There was another match I'll remember for the rest of my life, although it wasn't one I took part in. I had a friend in university whom I had talked into joining the gym. First he took judo, and he did quite well. Once there was a competition and he was fighting. He took a jump forward and landed headfirst on the mat. His vertebrae were dislocated and he was paralyzed. He died 10 days later in the hospital. He was a good guy. And to this day I regret talking him into taking judo. . . .

Traumas like this were quite frequent during the competitions and matches. People would break their arms or legs. Matches were a form of torture. And training was hard, too. We used to go to an athletic center outside of Leningrad on Khippiyarvi Lake. It's a fairly large lake, about 17 kilometers wide. Every morning when we got up, we ran around the lake first thing. After our run, there would be exercise, then training, breakfast, more workouts, lunch, rest after lunch, and then workouts again.

We used to travel around the country a lot. Once we went to a match in Moldavia, in preparation for the Spartakiad competition of the peoples of the USSR. It was horribly hot. I was coming out of our workout with my friend Vasya, and wine was for sale everywhere. He said to me, "Let's toss back a bottle of wine each." "It's too hot out," I replied. "Then let's just relax," he said. "Alright, alright. Let's get some wine," I said.

We each took a bottle, went back to our room, and flopped down on our beds. He opened his bottle. "It's too hot," I said. "I'm not going to." "Really?" he said. "Okay, have it your way." He gulped the bottle straight down. Then he looked at me. "Are you sure you aren't going to have any?" "I'm sure," I said. So he took the second bottle and knocked it back. He put the empty bottles on the table, and instantly he was out like a light. There he was, suddenly snoring. I really regretted not drinking along with him! I squirmed and squirmed. I couldn't hold out any longer, and poked him. "Hey, you. You're snoring, stop it! You're snoring like an elephant."

That was pretty much the exception. We didn't party much, because drinking made the workouts that much harder. There was this one huge guy that worked out with us. His name was Kolya. Not only was he gigantic, but he had this incredible face. He had a massive jaw that jutted forward and a huge overhanging brow. One night some hooligans started picking on him in a dark alley, and he said, "Guys, calm down. Pipe down for just a second." Then he took out a match, struck it, and held it up to his face. "Just look at me," he said. And that was the end of that incident.

Sergei Roldugin (soloist in the Mariinsky Theater Symphony Orchestra, a family friend of the Putins, and godfather of Putin's older daughter, Masha):

Volodya went to school with my brother. When I moved to Leningrad, my brother told me about Vovka. He brought him over to our house, and we hit it off. I think it was in 1977. After that, he became like a brother to me. When I had nowhere to go, I would go over to his house. I would eat and sleep there.

I was drafted into the army and served in Leningrad. Once, Vovka came over to see me in his Zaporozhets. I jumped over the fence and went AWOL. We went cruising around Leningrad all night. The muffler was broken, and we raced around, singing songs. I can even remember the song we sang:

"We had just one night,
Someone's train left this morning,
And then someone's plane a little later . . . "

We sang and sang, very loudly, without any inhibitions. After all, the muffler was broken.

Once my mother was given a state lottery ticket instead of change at a cafeteria, and she won a Zaporozhets car. I was in the third year of university and we couldn't decide what to do with that car for a long time, since we were living very modestly. I had just bought my first coat when I came back from working construction, a year after the vacation with my friends in Gagry. This was my first decent coat. Money was tight in our family, and to give the car to me was absolute madness. We could have sold it, after all, and gotten at least 3,500 rubles for it. That would have settled our family budget well in advance. But my parents decided to spoil me. They gave me the Zaporozhets. I lived the good life in that car. I used to drive it everywhere, even to my matches.

I was a pretty wild driver, but I was terrified of crashing the car. How would I ever repair it?

Once you did get into an accident, though. You ran over a man.

It wasn't my fault. He jumped in front of me or something. . . . Decided to put an end to his life. . . . I don't know what on earth he was doing. He was an idiot. He ran off after I hit him.

They say you chased him.

What? You think I hit a guy with my car and then tried to chase him down? I'm not a beast. I just got out of the car.

Are you able to remain calm in critical situations?

Yes, I remain calm. Even too calm. Later, when I went to intelligence school, I once got an evaluation, where they wrote the following as a negative character assessment: "A lowered sense of danger." That was considered a very serious flaw. You have to be pumped up in critical situations in order to react well. Fear is like pain. It's an indicator. If something hurts, that means something's wrong with your body. It's a sign. I had to work on my sense of danger for a long time.

Evidently you aren't a gambler?
No, I'm not a gambler.
Toward the end of university we went to military training camp. Two of my friends were there, one of whom had gone to Gagry with me. We spent two months there. It was much easier than the athletic camps, and we got really bored. The main source of entertainment was cards. Whoever won went to the village and bought milk from an old lady. I refused to play, but my friends didn't. And they lost everything quickly. When they had nothing left, they would come and plead for money. They were real gamblers. And I would ask myself, "Should I give them anything? They'll just lose it." And they would say, "Listen, your few kopecks won't save you anyway. Why not just give them to us." And I would say to them "Alright. After all, I have a lowered sense of danger," and hand over the cash.
Boy, did they make out like bandits! They couldn't lose for winning. And we went to buy milk from the lady every night.

University is a time for romances. Did you have any?
Who didn't? But nothing serious ... if you don't count that one time.

First love?
Yes. She and I even planned to tie the knot.

When did that happen?
About four years before I actually got married.

So it didn't work out?
That's right.

What got in the way?
Something. Some intrigue or other.

She married someone else?
Someone else? Yes, later.

Who decided that you wouldn't get married?
I did. I made the decision. We had already applied for a marriage license. Everything was ready. Our parents on both sides had bought everything—the ring, the suit, the wedding dress. . . . The cancellation was one of the most difficult decisions of my life. It was really hard. I felt like a real creep. But I decided that it was better to suffer then than to have both of us suffer later.

That is, you literally ran away and left her at the altar?
Almost. Except that I didn't run away. I told her the truth—as much of it as I considered necessary.

Do you not want to talk about it?
No, I don't. It's a complicated story. It's the way it was. It was really hard.

Do you have any regrets?
No.

Sergei Roldugin:

I liked his girlfriend, she was a pretty girl; a medical student with a strong character. She was a friend to him, a woman who would take care of him. But did she love him? I don't know. Lyuda, his wife—or Lyudik, as we call her—now, she really loves him.

I got along very well with that girl. I think her name was also Lyuda. She used to worry about his health. It wasn't just, "Oh, honey, how do you feel?" She would say, "Now, I can tell your stomach is hurting." I don't know what happened between them. He didn't tell me anything. He just said that it was all over. I think the falling-out was just between them, because their parents had agreed to the match.

Vovka suffered, of course. The thing is, we are both Libras and we take things like that very much to heart. And at that time I saw that he . . . that his . . . that he was a very emotional person but he simply could not express his emotions. I often used to tell him that he was terrible at making conversation. Why did he have such trouble talking?

Of course, he is Cicero now, compared to the way he talked back then. I used to explain to him, "You talk very quickly, and you should never talk so quickly." As a stage performer, I thought I could help him out. He had very strong emotions, but he could not put them into any form. I think his profession left its imprint on his speech. Now he speaks beautifully. Expansively, intelligibly, and with feeling. Where did he learn to do that?

So you didn't collaborate with the KGB while you were an undergraduate?

They didn't even try to recruit me as an agent, although it was a widespread practice at the time. There were many people who collaborated with the security agencies. The cooperation of normal citizens was an important tool for the state's viable activity. But the main point was the kind of basis this cooperation was established upon. Do you know what a "seksot" is?

It means secret colleague or collaborator.
    Right. But do you know why it has acquired such a negative connotation?

Because collaborators fulfilled a certain function.
    What function?

Ideological.
    Yes, ideological. They did political sleuthing. Everyone thinks that intelligence is interesting. Do you know that ninety percent of all the intelligence information is obtained from an agent's network made up of ordinary Soviet citizens? These agents decide to work for the interests of the state. It doesn't matter what this work is called. The important thing is upon which basis this cooperation takes place. If it is based on betrayal and material gain, that's one thing. But if it is based on some idealistic principles, then it's something else. What about the struggle against banditry? You can't do anything without secret agents.*

So when did you join the KGB?
    All those years in university I waited for the man at the KGB office to remember me. It seemed that he had forgotten about me. After all, I had gone to see him as a school kid. Who would've thought that I could have such spunk? But I recalled that they didn't like people to show their own initiative, so I didn't make myself known. I kept quiet.
    Four years passed. Nothing happened. I decided that the case was closed, and I began to work out different options for

*This segment of questions and answers was published in newspapers, but was not included in the Russian edition of Vladimir Putin's book, First Person. Several other passages from the interviews that were published only in newspapers are included in this English edition.

finding employment either in the special prosecutor's office
or as an attorney. Both are prestigious fields.

But then, when I was in my fourth year of university, a
man came and asked me to meet with him. He didn't say who
he was, but I immediately figured it out, because he said, "I
need to talk to you about your career assignment. I wouldn't
like to specify exactly what it is yet."

I picked up on it immediately. If they didn't want to say
where, that meant it was *there*.

We agreed to meet right in the faculty vestibule. He was
late. I waited for about 20 minutes. Well, I thought, what a
swine! Or was someone playing a prank on me? And I
decided to leave. Then suddenly he ran up, all out of breath.

"I'm sorry," he said.

I liked that.

"It's all arranged," he said. "Volodya, there's still a lot of
time, but how would you feel if you were invited to work in
the agencies?"

I didn't tell him that I had dreamed of this moment since I
was a schoolboy. I didn't tell him, because I remembered my
conversation in the KGB office long ago: "We don't take people who come to us on their own initiative."

**And when you agreed to work in the agencies, did you think
about 1937?**

To be honest, I didn't think about it at all. Not one bit. I
recently met up with some old colleagues from the KGB
Directorate—guys who I worked with at the very beginning—
and we talked about the same thing. And I can tell you what I
said to them: When I accepted the proposition from the Directorate's personnel department (actually, my recruiter turned
out to be an official in the subdivision that served the univer-
sities), I didn't think about the [Stalin-era] purges. My notion

of the KGB came from romantic spy stories. I was a pure and utterly successful product of Soviet patriotic education.

You knew nothing about the purges?
I didn't know much. Yes, of course, I knew about Stalin's cult of personality. I knew that people had suffered and that the cult of personality had been dismantled. . . . I wasn't completely naïve. Keep in mind that I was 18 when I went to university and that I graduated at age 23.

But those who cared to know, knew all about it.
We lived under the conditions of a totalitarian state. Everything was concealed. How deep was that cult of personality? How serious was it? My friends and I didn't think about that. So I went to work for the agencies with a romantic image of what they did.

But after that conversation in the vestibule, I heard nothing more. The man disappeared. And then there was a phone call; an invitation to the university's personnel department. Dmitry Gantserov—I can still remember his name—was the one to speak to me.

But there was almost a slipup at the employment commission. When they got to my name, a representative from the department of law said, "Yes, we're taking him into the bar." Then the agent who was monitoring the students' assignments suddenly woke up—he had been asleep somewhere in the corner. "Oh, no," he said. "That question has already been decided. We're hiring Putin to work in the agencies of the KGB." He said it right out loud like that, in front of the job-assignment commission.

And then several days later I was filling out all sorts of application forms and papers.

They told you they were hiring you to work in intelligence?

Of course not. It was all very systematic. They put it sort of like this: "We are proposing that you work in the field where we'll send you. Are you ready?" If the applicant was wishy-washy and said that he had to think about it, they would simply say, "Okay. Next!" And that person wouldn't have another chance. You can't pick your nose and say, "I want this and I don't want that." They can't use people like that.

You evidently said you were ready to work where they sent you?

Yes. Of course. And they themselves didn't even know where I would be working. They were just hiring new people. It's actually a routine matter, recruiting personnel and determining who should be sent where. I was made a routine offer.

Sergei Roldugin:

Vovka told me right away that he was working in the KGB. Practically right away. Maybe he was not supposed to do that. He told some people that he was working in the police. On the one hand, I treated these guys with caution, because I had had some run-ins with them. I had traveled abroad and knew that there were always people posing as inspectors or officials from the Ministry of Culture. You had to keep your mouth shut when you were around them.

I once told a colleague of mine, "Come on, they're normal, they're nice guys." And he said, "The more you talk to them, the more dirt they will have in your file at 4 Liteiny Street."*

I never asked Volodya about his work. Of course I was curious. But I remember once I decided to corner him and find out something about some special operation. I got nowhere.

---

* 4 Liteiny Street was the address of the KGB headquarters in Leningrad and currently houses the KGB's successor, the FSB (Federal Security Service).

Later I said to him, "I am a cellist. I play the cello. I could never be a surgeon. Still, I'm a good cellist. But what is your profession? I know, you're a spy. I don't know what that means. Who are you? What do you do?"

And he said to me, "I'm a specialist in human relations." And that was the end of our conversation. And he really did think that he was able to judge personalities. When I divorced my first wife, Irina, he said, "I predicted that that's exactly how it would turn out." I disagreed—you couldn't know what would happen between me and Irina from the start. But his comment made a big impression on me. I believed what he said: that he was a specialist in human relations.

Part 4

THE YOUNG SPECIALIST

After a stint in counterintelligence with some stodgy hard-liners, Putin is sent to the Andropov Red Banner Institute in Moscow for additional training. The officers quickly take notice of the smart and unflappable trainee. He's offered a spot in the most coveted of divisions: foreign intelligence. Meanwhile, he meets a stunning airline stewardess, Lyudmila. He impresses her with hard-to-come-by tickets for three nights at the theater, procured through his KGB connections. Their courtship lasts three years. They marry and are transferred on Putin's first assignment abroad: Dresden, East Germany.

At first they assigned me to the Secretariat of the Directorate, and then to the counterintelligence division, where I worked for about five months.

Was it like you imagined it would be? What you were expecting?

No, of course it wasn't what I had imagined. I had just come from university, after all. And suddenly I was surrounded by old men who had been in their jobs during those unforgettable times. Some of them were just about to go into retirement.

One time a group was drafting a scenario. I was invited to join the meeting. I don't remember the details, but one of the veteran agents said that the plan should be followed in such-and-such a way. And I piped up: "No, that's not right." "What do you mean?" he said, turning to me. "It's against the law," I said. He was taken aback. "What law?" I cited the law. "But we have instructions," he said. Once again I cited the law. The men in the room didn't seem to understand what I was talking about. Without a trace of irony, the old fellow said, "For us, instructions *are* the main law." And that was that. That's how they were raised and that's how they worked. But I simply couldn't do things that way. And it wasn't just me. Practically all my peers felt the same way.

For several months I went through the formalities and knocked off some cases. I was sent to agent training for six months. Our school in Leningrad wasn't too exceptional. My superiors believed I had mastered the basics but that I needed some field preparation. So I studied in Moscow, and then came back to Petersburg for about half a year in the counter-intelligence division.

What year was this?

What year? It was at the end of the 1970s. Now people say that was when Leonid Brezhnev was beginning to tighten the screws. But it was not very noticeable.

Did you join the Communist Party while you were at the KGB?

To join the intelligence service, you had to be a party member. There were no exceptions. That rule made for some strange episodes. For instance, if a person had worked in a security unit for less than a year and was transferred to another unit. In the interim period, he grew out of Komsomol age. It was impossible to admit him to the party because nobody could give him a recommendation. To receive a recommendation, you had to have worked with a unit for at least a year. Nobody knew this person for a period longer than a year, so nobody could recommend him for party membership. He was ineligible for the Komsomol because of his age and he couldn't be admitted to the party. An intelligence man has to be a party member, so he was dismissed from the security service. It's ridiculous, but it's true.

They say that security people didn't like party appointees.

That is true. Party appointees were disliked. People who joined the intelligence service after being full-time party officials invariably turned out to be good for nothings, loafers and careerists. There were all kinds, but they usually had overblown egos. They were brought from some mid-level party post immediately into a top post with the KGB. They envisioned themselves only as big directors, and they didn't want to be operatives. Naturally, they always caused resentment among the professionals.

What other things caused resentment among the professionals?
I know for a fact that they resented it when non-establishment artists were harassed. In Moscow they used bulldozers to sweep away paintings. I still don't understand who came up with the idea—some member of an ideological department in the regional or central party committees. The KGB objected, saying that it was a stupid thing to do, but some guy in the ideological department of the Central Comittee in Moscow put his foot down for reasons I can't understand. I guess he was just conservative. And because the KGB was a highly regarded division of the party, they had to do as the party told them.

Did you always think along these lines?
For better or for worse, I was never a dissident. My career was shaping up well. But you know, a lot of things that our law-enforcement agencies began indulging in since the 1990s were absolutely impossible back then. Things were stricter. I'll give you an example. Let's say a group of dissidents were gathering in Leningrad for some kind of protest. Let's say it is timed to coincide with the birthday of Peter the Great. Dissidents in Peter generally timed their demonstrations to coincide with those sorts of dates. They also liked the anniversaries of the Decembrists.
They would think up some act of protest and then invite

diplomats and reporters in order to attract the attention of the international community. What could we do? We couldn't disperse them because we had no orders to do so. So we would organize our own laying of the wreaths at exactly the same place where the reporters were supposed to gather. We would call in the regional party committee and the trade unions, and the police would rope everything off. Then we'd show up with a brass band. We would lay down our wreaths. The journalists and the diplomats would stand and watch for awhile, yawn a couple of times, and go home. And when they left, the ropes would come down and anyone who wanted to protest could. But they wouldn't get any attention.

Did you take part in that activity?

My group was not particularly involved in these activities.

How do you know the details, then?

Nobody made a secret of it. We met in the cafeteria and chatted openly about it. Why am I saying this? Because what the agents did was wrong, of course. They were a manifestation of a totalitarian state. But the way they did things was covert. It was considered indecent to be too obvious. Things were not always so crude.

And the Sakharov affair wasn't crude?*

The Sakharov affair was crude.

**Dr. Andrei Sakharov, a prominent Russian physicist and human rights campaigner, was kept under constant KGB surveillance and harassment in the 1970s and 1980 for his dissident activities. He was arrested for his outspoken criticism of the Soviet invasion of Afghanistan in 1980 and exiled without trial to the closed city of Gorky (now Nizhny Novgorod). Soviet President Mikhail Gorbachev released Dr. Sakharov from exile in 1986 and he was subsequently elected to the Soviet parliament, where he continued to criticize Soviet human rights violations and suppression of democracy until his death in 1989.*

Sergei Roldulgin:
Sometimes Vovka and I would go to the Philharmonic after work. He would ask me about the proper way to listen to a symphony. I tried to explain it to him. If you ask him about Shostakovich's Fifth Symphony, he can tell you a lot because he loved it terribly when he first heard it and I explained it to him. And then Katya and Masha took up music. I'm the one to blame for that.

I'm absolutely convinced that our lecturers with their highfalutin talk about music are wildly wrong. The propaganda for classical music is really missing the mark. I explained to Volodya what a normal person should see and hear. I would say, "Listen, the music has started. That's the peaceful life—they're building communism. You hear that chord, ta-ti, pa-pa? And now the fascistic theme is coming in. Look, there it goes—those brass instruments are playing. That theme will now grow. And there's the peaceful theme, from the beginning. The two will clash now, here and there, here and there." He just loved this terribly.*

Volodya has a very strong character. Let's say I was a better soccer player. I would lose to him anyway, simply because he's as tenacious as a bulldog. He would just wear me down. I would take the ball away from him three times and he would tear it away from me three times. He has a terribly intense nature, which manifests itself in literally everything. Don't forget: He was the judo champion for Leningrad in 1976.

Once, right before Volodya went to Germany, we went to visit our friend Vasya Shestakov at a sports camp. Vasya was a coach for young kids. We got there at night, and he showed us some cots where we could get some sleep. In the morning, the kids from the camp woke up and said, "Hey, look at those two guys. We can take them, no sweat."

The boys went to work out on the mats. They were practicing judo. And Vasya said to Volodya, "Do you want to fight?" Volodya answered, "What, are

Shostakovich's Fifth Symphony was written in 1937, at the height of Stalin's Great Terror, when millions were being summarily executed or deported to hard labor. The composer's "Lady Macbeth of the Mtinsk District" had been attacked in Pravda (a government newspaper) in 1936. The Fifth Symphony was interpreted as Shostakovich's response to the threats against him and the purges of his associates.

you kidding? I haven't stood on a mat for years." So I pitched in: "Come on! What's wrong with you? Those kids said they could take us with no sweat. . . ." And Vasya kept egging him on. "Alright, alright," Volodya finally said. "You talked me into it." He needed a kimono, and he went up to a kid and said, "Listen, will you lend me your robe to fight in?" The kid said rudely, "Take somebody else's." So Volodya borrowed somebody else's kimono and came out onto the mat. The rude kid was his opponent. Vovka flipped that kid so fast that he earned a clear victory right away. Vasya took the microphone and announced, "And the winner is the master Vladimir Putin, 1976 Leningrad champion!" Volodya took the robe off, gave it back, and calmly walked away. I turned to the kid and said, "You're lucky I'm not the one who was fighting you!"

Once, at Eastertime, Volodya called me to go to see a religious procession. He was standing at the rope, maintaining order, and he asked me whether I wanted to go up to the altar and take a look. Of course I agreed. There was such boyishness in this gesture—"nobody can go there, but we can." We watched the procession and then headed home. We were waiting at a bus stop, and some people came up to us. Not thugs, but students who had been drinking. "Can I bum a cigarette off you?" one of them asked. I kept silent, but Vovka answered, "No, you can't." "What are you answering that way for?" said the guy. "No reason," said Volodya.

I couldn't believe what happened next. I think one of them shoved or punched Volodya. Suddenly somebody's socks flashed before my eyes and the kid flew off somewhere. Volodya turned to me calmly and said, "Let's get out of here." And we left. I loved how he tossed that guy! One move, and the guy's legs were up in the air.

During my six months in counterintelligence training, the officers from foreign intelligence began to notice me. They wanted to talk. First one conversation, then another, then a third and a fourth. . . Intelligence is always looking for people for themselves, including people from the security agencies. They took people who were young and had certain appropriate qualities.

Of course I wanted to go into foreign intelligence. Everyone did. We all knew what it meant to be able to travel abroad under the conditions of the Soviet Union. And espionage was considered the white-collar job in the agencies. There were many people who exploited their position in order to trade in foreign goods. It was an unfortunate fact.

Naturally, I agreed to go into intelligence, because it was interesting. I was sent for special training in Moscow, where I spent a year. Then I returned to Leningrad and worked for awhile in the "first department," as we used to call it. The first chief directorate is intelligence. It had subdivisions in all the large cities of the Soviet Union, including Leningrad. I worked there for about four and a half years, and then I went to Moscow for training at the Andropov Red Banner Institute, which is now the Academy of Foreign Intelligence.

Mikhail Frolov (retired colonel, instructor of the Andropov Red Banner Institute):
I worked at the Red Banner Institute for 13 years. Vladimir Putin came to me from the Leningrad Directorate of the KGB with the rank of major.

I decided to try him out in the role of division leader. At the Red Banner Institute, division leader was not just some sort of illustrious title. A lot depends on the division leader. You need organizational abilities, a certain degree of tact, and a businesslike manner. It seemed to me Putin had all that. He was a steady student, without slips. There were no incidents. There was no reason to doubt his honesty and integrity.

I remember he once came to my lecture wearing a three-piece suit, despite the fact that it was 30 degrees Celsius on the street. I was sitting in a short-sleeved shirt in the heat. Putin thought he had to appear in a business suit. I even pointed him out as an example to the others: "Look at Comrade Platov, now!" At the Institute, we didn't use students' real names. That's why

Putin wasn't Putin, but Platov. As a rule we usually kept the first letter of some-one's name. When I went to intelligence school, I was called Filimonov.

At the Red Banner, we didn't just teach the rules of intelligence and counterintelligence. We needed to study our trainees—their professional worth and personal qualities. We had to determine, in the final analysis, whether a trainee was suitable for work in intelligence.

The training at our institute was a kind of testing ground. I taught the art of intelligence, for example. What does intelligence mean? It's the ability to come into contact with people, the ability to select the people you need, the ability to raise the questions that are of interest to our country and our leaders, the ability to be a psychologist, if you will. So we had to study each trainee care-fully. We needed to be as sure of him as we were of our own right hand. At the end of the course, we wrote an evaluation of each graduate, which would determine his fate.

We asked all the teachers, from the counterintelligence department to the physical education department, to write their opinion of the trainees on paper. Their reports were sent to the head of the training department, who synthe-sized all this material and added his own observations, writing an exhaustive, detailed evaluation of each candidate.

It was hellish work. Each evaluation consisted of only four typewritten pages, but everything had to be covered—personal as well as professional qualities. We closed for a week or two, and sat and wrote and wrote. At the end of each evaluation we wrote our conclusion about the suitability or unsuit-ability of each graduate for work in intelligence.

One time we had a trainee who performed our assignments like clock-work. His fine analytical mind helped him to find the best solutions quickly. In fact, he was so quick that you sometimes had the impression that he knew the answer even before you asked him a question. But the ability to solve problems in and of itself is not the highest priority. At the end of his study I wrote an evaluation that prevented him from working in intelligence. Unfortu-nately, his personal qualities—his careerism and his lack of sincerity toward his comrades—disqualified him immediately.

For this particular trainee, the evaluation was like a lightning bc blue. The evaluation was positive on the whole, but it definitively blocked his way to a job in intelligence. He was not going to get a residency as an agent. I had worked in residencies myself, so I knew what could happen if a boy like this one wound up there. He would start quarrels and create a tense and nasty atmosphere, which would prevent people from working productively. So I had to write a negative evaluation.

As for Vladimir Vladimirovich [Putin], I can't say he was a careerist. But I do remember that I wrote about several negative characteristics in his evaluation. It seemed to me that he was somewhat withdrawn and uncommunicative. By the way, that could be considered both a negative and a positive trait. But I recall that I also cited a certain academic tendency among his negative aspects. I don't mean that he was dry. No, he was sharp-witted and always ready with a quip.

A very high-ranking graduate commission would then determine how each trainee would be used. After reading his evaluation, the commission would summon each graduate, examine him, and determine which division of the KGB he would be assigned to. As a result of this training, Vladimir Vladimirovich was assigned to KGB representation in the German Democratic Republic [GDR, or East Germany].

When I studied at the Red Banner, it was clear from the very beginning that I was being prepared for Germany because they pushed me to take German. It was just a question of where—the GDR or the FRG [Federal Republic of Germany], East or West.

In order to go to the FRG, you had to work in the appropriate department of the central office of the KGB. You had to stick it out for a year or two, or three. It depended on the person. That was one option. Could I have done that? Sure, in theory.

The second option was to go immediately to the GDR. And I decided it was better to travel right away.

Were you married at the time?

Yes.

Once, when I was working in the first department in Peter, a friend of mine called me and invited me to the theater to see a performance by Arkady Raikin, the comic. He had tickets, and he said there would be girls there. We went, and there really were girls.

The next day we went back to the theater. I got tickets this time. And then we went a third time. I began to date one of the girls. We got to be friends. She was Lyuda, my future wife.

And how long did you date?

For a long time. About three years, probably. I was 29, and I was used to planning every move. But my friends started saying, "Listen, that's enough, you should get married."

They were probably envious.

Of course they were. But I knew that if I didn't get married in the next two or three years, I never would. I had gotten used to the bachelor's life, but Lyudmila changed all that.

Lyudmila Putina (Putin's wife):

I'm from Kaliningrad. I worked as a stewardess on domestic flights. There were no international flights to Kaliningrad. After all, it was a closed city. Our flight crew was small and young.

My girlfriend and I flew to Leningrad for three days. She was also a stewardess on our crew, and she invited me to the Lensoviet Theater, to a performance by Arkady Raikin. She had been invited by a boy, but she was afraid to go by herself, so she invited me along. When the boy heard that she was inviting me, he brought Volodya.

The three of us—myself, my girlfriend, and her friend—met on Nevsky

Prospect, near the Duma building, where there is a theater ticket office. Volodya was standing on the steps of the ticket office. He was very modestly dressed. I would even say he was poorly dressed. He looked very unprepossessing. I wouldn't have paid any attention to him on the street.

We watched the first hour of the show. During the intermission we went to the buffet. We had a good time, and I tried to make everyone laugh. But I was no Raikin—nobody was reacting to me much. Still, I wasn't discouraged.

After the show we agreed to meet again and go to the theater. My girlfriend and I had come for only three days, and we wanted to see a lot of a cultural things, of course. We understood that Volodya was the kind of person who could get tickets to any theater.

We met up again the next day, although the friend who had introduced us didn't come.

Sergei Roldugin:

I bought my first car, a Zhiguli, the original model. I had just finished the conservatory and landed a job in Mravinsky's Collective. We toured Japan and all the rest. I had more money than Vovka. I would bring him souvenirs from my trips—T-shirts and the like.

Once, we agreed to meet on Nevsky. He said, "Two girls will come up to you and say they're with me. I'll be there within 15 minutes, and then we'll go to the theater." The girls arrived on time, just as agreed. One of them was Lyuda. She was very nice. We got into the Zhiguli and began to wait for him. At first, I felt terribly uncomfortable sitting with them. Some friends of mine passed by and recognized me, and it was all rather unfortunate. We sat there for about an hour. I spent the whole time exhausting these girls with conversation, or so it seemed to me.

Finally, Volodya appeared. He was always late, by the way. We went to the theater. I don't remember what we saw, of course. No idea. I only remember those friends who passed by and recognized me.

Lyudmila Putina:

On the second day we went to the Leningrad Music Hall, and on the third day to the Lensoviet Theater. Three days, three theaters. On the third day, it was time to say goodbye. We were in the metro. Volodya's friend stood off to one side. He knew that Volodya was the kind of person who didn't readily give out information about himself, much less his home telephone number. But he noticed that Volodya was handing me his telephone number. After I left, he said to Volodya, "What, have you gone mad?" Volodya never did things like that.

Did your husband tell you that?

Of course.

And did he tell you where he worked?

He did: in the criminal investigation department of the police. And then later, I learned that he was in the KGB, in foreign intelligence. For me, at that time, it didn't matter, whether it was the KGB or the police. Now I know the difference.

I told her that I worked in the police. That was the identity that security agents, especially those in intelligence, would use as a cover. If you blabbed about where you worked, you wouldn't be sent abroad. Almost everybody had an ID from the criminal investigation office. I did, too. And that's what I told her. Who knew how our relationship was going to turn out?

Lyudmila Putina:

During that first trip, I fell in love with Leningrad at first sight. It was because I had such a good time. A city seems nice and pleasant to you when you meet nice people there.

But did you fall in love with this unprepossessing, modestly dressed guy?

I fell in love later, and fell hard. But not right away. At first, I just called him up.

And you, as a nice girl, didn't give him your telephone number?

I didn't have a telephone in Kaliningrad. At first I called him, then I began to fly to Leningrad for dates. How do most people travel for dates? On a tram, or a bus, or a taxi. But I flew to my dates.

The Kaliningrad crew did not have any flights to Leningrad. So I was given three or four days off, and I flew on an ordinary passenger flight. There was something about Volodya that attracted me. Within three or four months, I had decided that he was the man for me.

Why? You yourself said he was plain and dull.

Perhaps it was his inner strength, the same quality that draws everybody to him now.

Did you want to get married?

Just for the sake of getting married? No, never. But to marry Volodya—yes.

But you only got married three and a half years later. What did you do all that time?

I spent three and a half years courting him!

How did he finally make up his mind?

One night we were sitting at his house, and he said, "You know what kind of person I am by now. In general I'm not

very easygoing." He was being self-critical. He explained that
he was the silent type; that he was rather abrupt in some
things and could even insult people, and so on. He was saying
that he was a risky life partner. And he added: "In three and a
half years, you have probably made up your mind."

It sounded to me like we were breaking up. "Yes, I've
made up my mind," I said. He let out a doubtful "Yes?" Then
I was sure that that was it, we were breaking up. But then he
said, "Well, then, if that's the way it is, I love you and pro-
pose that we get married." So it all came as a complete surprise to me.

I agreed. Three months later we were married. We had our
wedding on a floating restaurant, a little boat tied up to the
riverbank.

We took this event very seriously. You can tell from our
wedding portrait that we were both super-serious. For me,
marriage was not a step taken lightly. And for him, too. There
are people who take a responsible attitude toward marriage.

**And did he, as a person who was responsible and reliable,
plan where you were going to live?**

There was nothing to plan. We lived with his parents, in a
27-meter-square apartment—a boathouse, as we used to call
them then. You know the kind, with the high windowsills? It
was very hard to exchange it for another. Only one of the
rooms had a balcony, and the windows in the kitchen and
the other room were way up near the ceiling. When you sat at
the table, you couldn't see the street outside, only the wall in
front of your eyes. It was a big minus when you were trying
to trade.

Volodya's parents lived in the 15-meter-square room with

the balcony. Our room, the one with no balcony, was 12 square meters. The apartment itself was in a district of newly constructed apartment blocks called Avtovo. Volodya's father had received the apartment as a disabled war veteran.

Did you get along well with his parents?

Yes. His parents treated me like the woman who had been chosen by their son. And he was their sun, moon, and stars. They did everything they could for him. No one could do more for him than they did. They invested their whole lives in him. Vladimir Spiridonovich and Maria Ivanovna were very good parents.

And how did he treat them?

Enviably. He treated them so kindly. He never offended them. Of course, on occasion they would be dissatisfied with something and he wouldn't agree with them, but in that sort of situation he would hold his tongue rather than cause them pain.

How did you two get along in the early years?

The first year we were married, we lived in total harmony. There was a continuous sense of joy, as though we were on holiday. Then I got pregnant with our oldest daughter, Masha. She was born when I was in my fourth year of school, and Volodya left for a year to study in Moscow.

You didn't see each other all that time?

I visited him once a month in Moscow. And he came to visit two or three times. It was impossible for him to come more often.

Sergei Roldugin:

One day he came from Moscow for a few days and somehow he managed to break his arm. Some punk was bugging him in the metro, and he socked the guy. The result was a broken arm. Volodya was very upset. "They're not going to understand this in Moscow. I'm afraid there are going to be consequences," he said. And there really was some unpleasantness, but he didn't tell me any of the details. Everything turned out okay in the end.

Lyudmila Putina:

His training led to a trip to Germany. He was supposed to go to Berlin, but then a friend of Volodya's recommended him to the station chief in Dresden. The friend was also a Leningrader and worked in Dresden. His tour of duty was coming to an end, so he recommended Volodya for the job. The job in Berlin was considered more prestigious and the work was apparently more interesting, since it involved travel to West Berlin. In fact, I never learned the facts, and Volodya would never tell me. We never had a conversation on this topic.

Sergei Roldugin:

They suited one another in all respects. Of course, she began to display some temper later on. She isn't afraid of speaking the truth. And she isn't afraid to talk about herself. Once I bought a rocking chair and couldn't fit it into the trunk of my car, no matter how I tried. She started giving me advice: "You have to turn it this way, and not that . . ." But there was no way it was going to fit into the car, and it was heavy, to boot. I said, "Lyuda, be quiet." She almost went into hysterics. "Why are you men all so stupid?" she yelled.

Lyuda is an excellent hostess. Whenever I came to visit, she always whipped something up fast. She's a real woman, who could stay up all night having a good time, and still clean up the apartment and cook the next morning. . . .

Lyuda is five years younger than me. Before becoming a stewardess, she studied at a technical college. She dropped out during her third year. She was trying to decide where to

go, when she and I met. She wanted advice on where to go to
school. I said she should go to the university. She decided to
apply to the philology faculty, first to the preparatory department. Then she went to the Spanish department and began to
take languages. She learned two languages, Spanish and
French. They also taught Portuguese there, but she didn't
study that much. And when we went to Germany, she learned
to speak German fluently.

Sergei Roldugin:

Before they left for Germany, Masha was born. My former father-in-law
had a dacha near Vyborg, a wonderful place, and after we picked Lyuda up
from the maternity hospital we all went out there and spent some time
together—Volodya, Lyuda, my wife, and I. Of course, we celebrated the birth of
Masha. We had dances in the evenings. "Hold the thief, hold the thief, it's time
to catch him!" Vovka could move well, although he didn't seem particularly
good at ballroom dancing.

Before we left for Germany, they had to put Lyudmila
through a security clearance. They began this process while I
was studying in Moscow. At that point I still didn't know
where I would be posted; but wherever it was, it would place
stringent demands on my family members. For example,
one's wife had to be in good health and be able to work in a
hot and humid climate. Imagine you've gone through five
years of training, and then, when you're finally ready to go
abroad, into the field, to work, your wife can't go due to poor
health. That would be terrible!

They checked Lyudmila out thoroughly. They didn't tell
her about it, of course. They called her into the university
personnel department when it was all over, and reported that
she had passed the special clearance procedure. So we went to
Germany.

Part 5

THE SPY

Though the standard of living is high and the beer is good, the Putins find East Germany a backward place. The country seems stuck in a totalitarian state that Russia left three decades before. Putin is shocked by the atmosphere of fear and stagnation. Then the Berlin Wall falls and chaos breaks out. Mobs ransack the Stasi headquarters. They surround the KGB offices. Panicked, Putin calls for military backup, but receives this ominous answer, "Moscow is silent." He suddenly feels as though everything is falling apart, as though the Soviet Union has simply disappeared.

You came to the KGB in 1975 and resigned in 1991. Sixteen years. How many of them did you spend abroad?

Not even a full five. I worked only in the GDR, in Dresden. We went there in 1985 and left after the fall of the Berlin Wall, in 1990.

Did you want to go abroad?

I did.

But the KGB was working officially in the GDR and the other socialist countries. As one of your former colleagues said, the GDR is a province, from the perspective of foreign intelligence-gathering.

Probably. Actually, from that perspective, Leningrad is also a province. But I was always quite successful in these provinces.

But this wasn't like *The Sword and Shield*, was it? What about the romance of intelligence?

Don't forget that by that time, I had already worked in the agencies for 10 years. How romantic do you think that was?

Intelligence was always the fanciest organization in the

KGB. The agents lived abroad for years. You could spend three years in a capitalist country or four to five in the so-called socialist camp. Then you'd go for nine months of retraining in Moscow and go abroad once again. I have a friend who worked in Germany for 20 years and another who worked there for 25 years. When you come home for nine months between trips, you don't fully integrate back into life. When you come home from serving abroad, it's hard to get used to our reality. You're more aware of what's going on. We young people would talk with our older colleagues. I don't mean the really old ones who remember the Stalin era, but people with work experience. And they were a generation with entirely different views, values, and sentiments.

One of my friends worked in Afghanistan as head of a security group. When he returned home, we grilled him a lot. Do you remember what it was like here then? Everything that was connected to Afghanistan was a constant "Hurrah!" We all felt very patriotic. So we talked to him, and I asked him how he felt about his work in Afghanistan. You see, his signature was required for missile launchings. Without his signature, the decision to bomb would not be made. His answer to my question came as a shock to me: "You know, I judge the results of my work by the number of documents that I did not sign." That really stunned me. After conversations like that, you start to think and rethink things. A person we respected was saying this. These people were authorities in the best sense of the word. And suddenly their opinion was at odds with the customary, established clichés. In intelligence at that time, we were allowed to think differently. And we could say things that few normal citizens could permit themselves to say.

Lyudmila Putina:

We arrived in Dresden in 1986. I had graduated from university by that time. Masha was a year old and, we were expecting a second child. Katya was born in Dresden. I only knew the German I had learned in school, no more.

I did not receive any special instructions before the trip. I just went through a medical exam and that was it. Our people worked completely legally in the GDR, after all. We lived in the building that housed the German state security, the Stasi. Our neighbors knew where we worked, and we knew where they worked. Although perestroika had already begun in the USSR, they still believed in the bright future of communism.

What did you do in Germany?

The work was political intelligence—obtaining information about political figures and the plans of the potential opponent.

Is it correct to say you were involved in "intelligence from the territory"?

More or less, although that phrase generally means foreign intelligence-gathering from the territory of the USSR [about other countries], and we were working from the territory of East Germany. We were interested in any information about the "main opponent," as we called them, and the main opponent was considered NATO.

Did you travel into West Germany?

No, not once while I was working in the GDR.

So what exactly did you do there?

The usual intelligence activities: recruiting sources of information, obtaining information, analyzing it, and sending it to Moscow. I looked for information about political parties, the tendencies inside these parties, their leaders. I examined today's leaders and the possible leaders of tomorrow and the promotion of people to certain posts in the parties and the government. It was important to know who was doing what and how, what was going on in the Foreign Ministry of a particular country, how they were constructing their policy on certain issues and in various areas of the world, and how our partners would react in disarmament talks. Of course, in order to obtain such information, you need sources. So recruitment of sources, procurement of information, and assessment and analysis were big parts of the job. It was very routine work.

Lyudmila Putina:

We did not discuss work at home. I think the nature of my husband's work made a difference. There was always a principle at the KGB: Do not share things with your wife. They told us that there had been incidents when excessive frankness had led to unfortunate consequences. They always proceeded from the premise that the less the wife knew, the better she'd sleep. I socialized fairly often with the Germans, and if one of my acquaintances was undesirable, Volodya would let me know.

Life in the GDR was probably better than in Peter?

Yes, we had come from a Russia where there were lines and shortages, and in the GDR there was always plenty of everything. I gained about 25 pounds, and weighed about 165.

And how much do you weigh now?

165.

What happened?
Let me tell you honestly . . .

The beer?
Of course! We used to go to a little town called Radeberg, where there was one of the best breweries in East Germany. I would order a three-liter keg. You pour the beer into the keg, you add a spigot, and you can drink straight from the barrel. So I had 3.8 liters of beer every week. And my job was only two steps from my house, so I didn't work off the extra calories.

And no sports?
There were no facilities there. And we also worked a lot.

Lyudmila Putina:
We lived in a service apartment in a German building. It was large, with 12 entryways. Our group took up five apartments. Volodya's driver and his wife lived in another building. And there were four other apartments with military intelligence nearby. All the rest were Germans who worked at the GDR state security.

Our group worked in a separate building—a German mansion that was surrounded by a wall. It had either three or four flours, I don't remember. But it was only a five-minute walk from our apartment to that building. From the window of his office, Volodya could see little Katya in day care. In the morning he would take Masha to the day-care center, which was right under the windows of our apartment, and then take Katya to the nursery.

They always came home for lunch. All of the guys would have lunch at home. Sometimes they would come to our house in the evenings—friends from work, sometimes Germans too. We were friends with several families. It was fun. We talked about nothing special, told jokes and anecdotes. Volodya knows how to tell a joke well.

On the weekends we would take trips outside the city. We had a service car, a Zhiguli. This was considered a pretty good car in the GDR, at least compared to the local Trabants. Getting a car in those days in the GDR was as difficult as it was in the Soviet Union. So, on the weekends, we would take trips with the whole family. There were many beautiful places outside Dresden. Saxony was only 20 to 30 minutes away. We would take a walk, have some hot dogs and beer, and then head home.

You had some evident successes when you worked in Dresden.

My work went well. It was normal to be promoted while working at a foreign posting. I was promoted twice.

What was your job title when you came to the GDR?

I was a senior case officer. My next job was assistant to the head of the department. That was considered quite a good advance. And then I was promoted to senior assistant. There was nothing higher. Above me was the top managerial level, and we only had one boss. So as an incentive, I was made a member of the Party committee of the KGB representation in the GDR.

There are reports that you took part in an operation called Lightbeam.

I don't know, exactly. I wasn't involved in it. I don't even know if it was executed or not. As far as I can remember, it involved working with the political leadership of the GDR. I didn't have anything to do with it.

But people say that you were the one who controlled the former secretary of the Dresden regional committee of the SED, Hans Modrow.*

I met Modrow a few times at official receptions. That was the extent of our acquaintance. He socialized with people of a different rank—the commander of the army, our senior communications officer. And, in general, we didn't work with Party functionaries. Including our own, by the way. It was prohibited.

And you weren't the one to obtain the documentation about the Eurofighter bomber?

I wasn't involved in technical intelligence. I didn't do that line of work. Why have they made up so much about me? It's complete nonsense!

Well, they wanted to portray you as a super-spy. And you're denying everything. But then why did you get promoted?

For concrete results in my work—that's what it was called. Success was measured by the quantity of realized units of information. If you procured information from the sources you had at your disposal, put it together, and sent it to the relevant offices, you would obtain the appropriate evaluation.

You are answering like an intelligence officer. In other words, you're not really answering. Take Markus Wolf, the former head of East German intelligence. He insulted you. He says

In the fall of 1989, Hans Modrow was secretary of the Communist Party (SED) in Dresden and responsible for "emergency situations" while large, peaceful, anti-GDR demonstrations were taking place there nightly. He refrained from suppressing the antigovernment demonstrations and was made prime minister at the height of the agitation against the Communist government (1989–1990). His government and party were soundly defeated in the momentum for German reunification.

that the bronze medal that you received, with the inscription "For services to the National People's Army of the GDR," is a medal that they gave to practically every secretary, provided she didn't have any gross violations in her record.

Markus Wolf is entirely correct. And there is nothing offensive in what he said. Just the opposite. He just confirmed that I didn't have any gross violations in my record. The only thing is that my medal, I believe, doesn't say "for services" but says "for outstanding services to the National People's Army of the GDR."

You're not expecting any sensational publications about yourself, for example, in Germany?

No. To be honest, no.

It's kind of funny to read all that nonsense in the papers. I'm baffled to read that the Western countries are looking for agents whom I recruited. It's all baloney. Our friends, as we called the GDR security agents, have copies of everything we produced. It is all preserved in their archives. Therefore it is impossible to say that I was involved in some sort of secret operations that were out of sight of the local GDR government agencies or the security agencies. A large part of our work was done through citizens of the GDR. They are all on the roster. Everything is transparent and understandable. And German counterintelligence knows about all of this.

I did not work against the interests of Germany. That's absolutely obvious. Moreover, if it had been otherwise, I wouldn't have been allowed to visit any Western country. I wasn't a high-ranking official then. But I have traveled a lot of places since then, including Germany. Some of the GDR state security officers even wrote letters to me when I worked in St. Petersburg as vice mayor. And at a reception I once said to the German consul, "Please note that I receive letters, and that these are my personal connections. I understand that you have a campaign now against former state security agents. They are being captured and persecuted for political reasons. But these are my friends, and I will not renounce them." He replied, "We understand everything, Mr. Putin. Everything is clear." They knew perfectly well who I was and where I had come from. I didn't hide it.

Lyudmila Putina:
Of course life in the GDR was very different from life in Russia. The streets were clean. They would wash the windows once a week. There was an abundance of goods—not like what they had in West Germany, of course, but still better than in Russia. There was one detail that surprised me. It was trivial—should I even mention it? It was the way German women would hang out their clothes. In the morning, before work, about 7:00 A.M., they would go out in the backyard. And each housewife would stretch a rope between these metal poles, and then she would hang her laundry out on the lines in very, very neat rows, with clothespins. They were all alike.

The Germans were very orderly in their daily life, and their standard of living was better than ours. I think the GDR state security people got higher salaries than our guys, judging from how our German neighbors lived. Of course we tried to economize and to save up enough money to buy a car. Then, when we returned home, we bought a Volga. Some of Volodya's salary was paid in German marks and some in dollars. But we did not spend much money, except on food. We didn't have to spend any money on anything. We lived in a government apartment with government-issued dishes.

Really, we sat on our suitcases and dreamed of returning home. At the beginning, we were really homesick. But we were pretty comfortable in the GDR. Four years passed, and in four years a foreign country and a foreign city can become almost like your own. When the Berlin Wall fell and it was clear this was the end, we had the horrible feeling that the country that had almost become our home would no longer exist.

If German counterintelligence, as you say, knows everything about your activity in the GDR, then that means that it knows about everything and everyone you worked with in your intelligence group. Your entire agents' network is ruined.

We destroyed everything—all our communications, our lists of contacts and our agents' networks. I personally burned a huge amount of material. We burned so much stuff that the furnace burst.

We burned papers night and day. All the most valuable items were hauled away to Moscow. But it no longer meant anything in terms of operations. All of the contacts were cut off. Work with the information sources was stopped for security reasons. The materials were destroyed or sent into the archives. Amen!

When was that?

In 1989, when they began to break into the directorate of the Ministry of Security in the GDR. We were afraid they would come for us, too.

But you can understand the people who broke into the Ministry of Security, can't you?

You can. Only the way in which they expressed their protest was upsetting.

I stood in the crowd and watched it happen. People were breaking into the Ministry of Security (MGB). A woman shouted: "Look for the passageway under the Elba! There are

prisoners there being tortured in water up to their knees!"
What prisoners? Why under the Elba? True, there was a jail
cell used for interrogations, but obviously it wasn't under the
Elba.

This was a backlash, of course. I understood those people—they were tired of being watched by the MGB, especially
because the surveillance was so totally invasive. They saw the
MGB as a monster.

But the MGB was also part of society. It was infected with
the same sicknesses. There were all kinds of people who
worked there, but the people I knew were decent people. I
was friends with many of them, and I think that the way they
are now being castigated isn't right. It's the same thing the
MGB system did to the civil society of East Germany, to its
people.

Yes, there probably were some MGB agents who engaged
in persecution of people. I didn't see it. I don't want to say
that it didn't happen. But I personally did not see it.

In a sense, the GDR was a real eye-opener for me. I
thought I was going to an Eastern European country, to the
center of Europe. It was already the end of the 1980s. And
suddenly, when I talked with people from the MGB, I realized
that both they themselves and the GDR were going through
something the Soviet Union had gone through many years
before.

It was a harshly totalitarian country, similar to the Soviet
Union, only 30 years earlier. And the tragedy is that many people sincerely believed in all those Communist ideals. I wondered at the time: if some changes in the USSR begin, how
would it affect the lives of these people? The alarmists got it
right. It was hard to imagine that such abrupt changes could
take hold in the GDR. No one could have ever imagined it!

And we didn't know how it would end. Of course we had begun to suspect that the regime would not last long. Perestroika had already begun in our country—many closed subjects were now being discussed openly. But in the GDR, that sort of talk was totally taboo—they were trying to totally preserve their society. Families had been torn apart. Some relatives lived on one side of the Wall, some on the other. Everyone was followed. Of course that wasn't normal. It wasn't natural.

But they didn't touch you when they broke into the MGB?
Well, crowds gathered around our building, too.

Alright, the Germans tore apart their own MGB. That was their own internal affair. But we weren't their internal affair. Those crowds were a serious threat. We had documents in our building. And nobody lifted a finger to protect us.

We were prepared to defend ourselves against the crowd, and we would have been within our rights to do so, under an agreement between our ministries and governments. We were forced to demonstrate our readiness to defend our building. And that determination certainly made an impression on them, at least for awhile.

Did you have bodyguards?
Yes, several.

You didn't try to go out and talk with people?
After a while, when the crowd grew angry, I went out and asked people what they wanted. I explained to them that this was a Soviet military organization. And someone shouted from the crowd: "Then why do you have cars with German license plates in the parking lot? What are you doing here, anyway?" It was as if they were saying, "We know what

you're up to." I explained that we had an agreement, which allowed us to use German license plates. "And who are you?" they shouted. "You speak German too well." I replied that I was a translator.

These people were in an aggressive mood. I called our group of forces and explained the situation. And I was told: "We cannot do anything without orders from Moscow. And Moscow is silent." After a few hours our military people did finally get there. And the crowd dispersed. But that business of "Moscow is silent"—I got the feeling then that the country no longer existed. That it had disappeared. It was clear that the Union was ailing. And it had a terminal disease without a cure—a paralysis of power.

Lyudmila Putina:

I saw what happened to my neighbors when all those revolutionary events started in the GDR. My neighbor, who was my friend, cried for a week. She cried for her lost ideals, for the collapse of everything that she had believed in her whole life. For them, it was the collapse of everything—their lives, their careers. They were all left without jobs. There was a ban on their profession. Katya had a teacher in the day-care center who was an educator by profession. After the fall of the Wall, she no longer had the right to work in day care and educate children. They had all been officers of the MGB. She went through a psychological crisis, but then somehow she pulled herself together and went to work in a home for senior citizens.

Another German friend from the GDR found a job with a Western firm. She had worked there for a long time and was quite successful, when suddenly her boss, in the midst of a heated discussion, said that all people from the GDR were dense, uneducated, and incompetent—that they were second-class citizens. She listened to all this and said, "But I'm from the GDR. Do you think I'm incompetent as well?" Her boss fell silent. He had no retort because there was nothing wrong with her work.

Did you suffer when the Berlin Wall fell?

Actually, I thought the whole thing was inevitable. To be honest, I only really regretted that the Soviet Union had lost its position in Europe, although intellectually I understood that a position built on walls and dividers cannot last. But I wanted something different to rise in its place. And nothing different was proposed. That's what hurt. They just dropped everything and went away.

Later, back in Peter, I had a very interesting meeting with Kissinger, and he confirmed what I already thought. There was a commission called the Kissinger-Sobchak Commission, founded to develop St. Petersburg and to attract foreign investment. Kissinger came to our city several times. Once I met him at the airport. We got into a car and went to the residence. On the way, he asked me where I was from and what I was doing. He was an inquisitive old fellow. He looks like he is nodding off to sleep, but in fact he sees and hears everything. We spoke through an interpreter. He asked me, "Have you worked here long?" I replied that it had been about a year. "Where did you work before that?" asked Kissinger.

"At the Leningrad City Council," I replied.

"And before the Leningrad City Council?"

"At the university."

"And before the university?"

"I was in the army before that."

"In what troops?"

"Well," I thought to myself. "Now I'm going to upset you, Mr. Kissinger."

"I worked in intelligence," I said.

"Did you work abroad?" he asked calmly.

"Yes," I said. "In Germany."

"East or West?"

"East."

"All decent people got their start in intelligence. I did, too," said Kissinger.

Then he said something that was completely unexpected and very interesting. "You know, I am very much criticized for the position I took regarding the USSR back then. I believed that the Soviet Union should not abandon Eastern Europe so quickly. We were changing the balance in the world very rapidly, and I thought it could lead to undesirable consequences. And now I'm being blamed for that position. People say, 'See, the Soviets left, and everything's normal. You thought it was impossible.' But I really did think it was impossible." Then he thought a while and added, "Frankly, to this day I don't understand why Gorbachev did that."

I had never imagined I might hear something like that from the lips of Henry Kissinger. I told him what I thought, and I will repeat it to you right now: Kissinger was right. We would have avoided a lot of problems if the Soviets had not made such a hasty exit from Eastern Europe.

Part 6

THE DEMOCRAT

Disillusioned with the KGB, Putin decides to embark on an academic career. He returns to Leningrad University intending to write his doctoral dissertation, but is persuaded to work for Anatoly Sobchak, the chair of the City Council, instead. He throws himself into politics. As Sobchak's deputy, he gets involved in the economic and political reconstruction of St. Petersburg and helps Sobchak in his bid to become mayor. But then things get rough. Lyudmila has a terrible car accident; their dacha is destroyed by fire; and Sobchak looses the mayoral elections. Putin resigns from the Council to plot his next move.

Did you ever think that the KGB had become obsolete?
I was offered a job in the central office in Moscow, but I turned it down. Why? I knew that there was no future to the system. The country didn't have a future. And it would have been very difficult to sit inside the system and wait for it all to collapse around me.

Sergei Roldugin:
I remember how confused and upset Volodya felt about the collapse of the whole intelligence network in Germany. He would say, "You just can't do that! How can you do that? I know that I can be wrong, but how can the most highly qualified professionals be mistaken?" He was very disenchanted. I said to him, "You know, Volodya, don't get me started." Then he said, "I'm going to leave the KGB!" And I said to him, "There's no such thing as a former intelligence agent."

Volodya spoke from the heart, and I believed him. But how can you escape the knowledge and information in your mind? You can stop working at this organization, but its worldview and way of thinking remain stuck in your head.

The work we did was no longer necessary. What was the point of writing, recruiting, and procuring information? Nobody at Moscow Center was reading our reports. Didn't we warn them about what was coming? Didn't we provide them with recommendations on how to act? There was no reaction. Who wants to work for nothing? To spend years of your life—what for?—just to get paid?

Let's say, for example, that my friends in scientific and technical intelligence paid several million dollars for some information about an important scientific discovery. It would have cost our country billions of dollars to independently develop the same project. My friends would procure this information and send it to the Center. People there would look at it and say, "Wonderful. Great information. Thanks. Kisses. We'll recommend you guys for medals." But then they wouldn't use the intelligence. They wouldn't even try, because the technical level of our industry simply didn't allow for it.

In short, when we returned from Germany in January 1990, I continued to work in the agencies, but I began to think quietly about a backup plan. I had two children, and I couldn't afford to throw everything away. What could I do?

Sergei Roldugin:

When Volodya came back from Germany, he told me that he had been offered a promotion in Moscow or Peter. We discussed which position would be better, and I said, "In Moscow, they're all bosses. There are no normal people there. One guy has an uncle in the ministry, another has a brother, a third has a brother-in-law. And you don't have anybody. How will you make it there?" Volodya thought for a while and then said, "But Moscow . . . there are prospects there." But I could see that he was clearly leaning toward staying in St. Petersburg.

I was happy to go "undercover" at Leningrad State University (LGU). I wanted to write my doctoral dissertation, check out the university, and perhaps get a job there. So in 1990, I became assistant to the president of the university, responsible for international liaison. I was in the "active reserves."

Lyudmila Putina:

We followed perestroika and were aware of everything that went on from 1986 to 1988, but only from television. We heard people's stories about the happy mood of those years.

But when we returned home, I didn't notice any changes—there were the same terrible lines, the ration cards, the coupons, the empty shelves. For a while after we returned home I was even afraid to go to the store. I wasn't able, like some people, to sniff out all the bargains and to stand in all the lines. I would just dart into the nearest store, buy whatever was most necessary, and go home. It was horrible.

Besides, we hadn't accumulated savings while working in Germany. The car ate up all our money. Our German neighbors did give us their old washing machine, a 20-year-old model. We brought it back home, and used it for five more years.

The situation changed for my husband at work. Despite the fact that, as far as I could tell, his work in Germany had been successful, he was clearly thinking about what to do next. I think at a certain point he felt that he had lost touch with his life's real purpose. And of course it wasn't easy, parting with the past and making the decision to go into politics.

At that time, the president of LGU was Stanislav Petrovich Merkuriev. He was a good man and a brilliant academic.

I began to write my dissertation, and chose Valery Abramovich Musin, one of the top specialists in international law, as my academic adviser. I chose a topic in the field of international private law and began to draft an outline for my work.

At the university, I reestablished contact with my old friends from the law faculty. Several of them had stayed on there, defended their dissertations, and become instructors and professors. One of them asked me to help Anatoly Sobchak, the chair of the Leningrad City Council. Sobchak needed someone good on his team. Apparently he was surrounded by crooks. Would I go and work for him? "You know, I have to think about it," I said. "I'm a KGB personnel officer, after all. And he doesn't know that. I could compromise him." "Just talk to him," my friend said.

I should note that by that time Sobchak was already a famous and popular person. I had followed him with great interest—followed what he did and said. True, I didn't like everything I saw, but he had gained my respect. It was even nicer that he'd been a teacher in the university where I had studied. Back when I was a student, I didn't have any personal connections to him. Some people have written that I was practically his favorite student. That's not true. He was just one of our lecturers for one or two semesters.

I met Anatoly Aleksandrovich Sobchak at his office in the Leningrad City Council. I remember the scene very well. I went in, introduced myself, and told him everything. He was an impulsive man, and said to me right off: "I'll speak to Stanislav Petrovich Merkuriev. Come to work starting Monday. That's it. We'll make the agreement right now, and you'll be transferred." I couldn't help but say, "Anatoly Aleksandrovich, I would be happy to do this. I am interested. But there is one circumstance that might be an obstacle to this transfer." "What?" he asked. I replied, "I must tell you that I am not just an assistant to the president, I'm also a staff officer of the KGB." He was silent for a moment. I must have really surprised him. He thought and thought, and then suddenly he said, "Well, screw it!"

Of course I wasn't expecting that reaction. This was our

very first personal encounter. He was a professor, a doctor of law, chair of the Leningrad City Council. I didn't expect such frank talk.

Then he said, "I need an assistant. Frankly, I'm afraid of going out into the reception area. I don't know who those people are."

The people in Sobchak's outer office—his closest cohorts—were harsh and rude in the best traditions of the Komsomol, the Soviet school. This disturbed the city council deputies and led to a conflict between Sobchak and the city council. Since I understood this, I told Anatoly Aleksandrovich that I would be happy to come and work for him, but that I would first have to tell my bosses at the KGB and resign from my post at the university.

This was a fairly delicate moment for me. It was difficult to tell my superiors that I intended to change jobs.

I went to my boss and said, "Anatoly Aleksandrovich is proposing that I leave the university and go to work for him. If it's impossible, I'm ready to resign." They replied: "No. Why? Go and work there. There's no question about it."

My superiors, who were fairly subtle people and understood the situation, did not try to impose any conditions on me. Therefore, although I was formally listed in the security agencies, I hardly ever set foot in the directorate building.

What's interesting is that the bosses never once tried to use me for any operations. I think they understood that it would have been pointless. Moreover, at that moment, everything, including the law-enforcement agencies, was falling apart.

Vladimir Churov (deputy chair of the Committee for Foreign Liaison of the St. Petersburg mayor's office):
Before 1991, the offices in Smolny were clearly divided. The big bosses

had two portraits hanging in their offices—of Lenin and Kirov—and those who were a rank below them had only Lenin's portrait. After they took the portraits down, empty hooks were left on the walls and everyone could pick what he wanted to hang in his office. Most guys selected a portrait of Yeltsin. Putin ordered himself a portrait of Peter the Great. Two portraits were brought to him for selection. One was a romantic painting of a young, curly-headed Peter wearing epaulettes; and the other—the one Putin chose—was an engraving. It was one of the last portraits of Peter the Great when his reforms were at their most active; right after the failed Prussian campaign and the Northern war, when Peter laid the foundations of the Russian Empire.

I think that Vladimir Vladimirovich chose that portrait of Peter on purpose. It was a rare and little-known picture. Peter looked rather mournful and preoccupied.

On one occasion my colleagues from the agencies tried to exploit my proximity to Sobchak. Sobchak used to go on business trips and was frequently out of town. He would leave me to run the office. One day he was in a big rush before a trip, and his signature was needed on a document. The document wasn't quite finished, but Sobchak couldn't wait for it. So he took three clean sheets of paper, put his signature at the bottom, and gave them to me, saying "Finish it up," and left.

That same evening my colleagues from the KGB came to see me. We spoke about this and that, and then they mentioned how great it would be to have Sobchak's signature on a certain document. Couldn't we discuss it? But I was a seasoned person—I had survived so many years without one slip-up—and I sized up the situation right away. I took out the folder and showed them the blank sheets of paper with Sobchak's signature. And they and I understood that this was testimony to the great degree of trust that Sobchak had in me.

"Can't you see that this man trusts me?" I said. "What do you want from me?" They immediately backed off. "No more questions," they said. "Sorry." And everything was nipped in the bud.

Still, it was an abnormal situation because, after all, I continued to get a salary from them, which, by the way, was more than I was getting at the city council. But soon circumstances arose that forced me to think about writing a letter of resignation.

Relations with the deputies in the city council were not always smooth, mostly because they lobbied someone's interests. Once a deputy came up to me and said, "You know, we have to help so-and-so. Could you do such and such?" I had already put him off several times. One day he said to me, "There are bad people here—all sorts of enemies—and they've sniffed out that you're a KGB agent. You have to foil them. I'm prepared to help you, but you have to do me a favor."

I realized that they wouldn't leave me alone. They would blackmail me, pure and simple. So I made a difficult decision and wrote my letter of resignation. I was just sick and tired of that brazen blackmail.

It was a very difficult decision for me. Although I had done virtually no work for the agencies in almost a year, my whole life was still tied up in them. Besides, it was 1990. The USSR hadn't collapsed yet. The August coup hadn't taken place. No one was sure about where the country was going. Sobchak was a prominent politician, but it was risky to tie my future to his. Everything might unravel at a moment's notice. And I also had a hard time imagining what I'd do if I lost my job at the mayor's office. I thought that if worse came to worst, I would go back to the university and finish my dissertation and earn some money somewhere part-time.

I had a stable spot in the agencies, and people treated me well. My life in the system had been full of successes. And still I wanted to leave. Why? I couldn't quite put my finger on it. It was the hardest decision of my life. I thought for a long time, collected myself, sat down, and in one quick draft, wrote my resignation letter.

After I turned in my resignation, I decided to announce publicly that I had worked in the security agencies. I turned to my friend Igor Abramovich Shadkhan, the film director, for help. He was a talented man. His most famous film was *Test for Adults*, and he worked in the television studio in Leningrad at that time. I came to him and said, "Igor, I want to speak openly about my professional past so that it stops being a secret and so that no one can blackmail me with it."

He taped an interview in which he asked me in detail about my work at the KGB, what I had done, when I had served in intelligence, and so on. The tape was shown on Leningrad television, and the next time someone came along hinting about my past, I immediately said, "That's enough. It's not interesting. Everyone already knows about that."

But my letter of resignation had gotten stalled somewhere. Somebody, somewhere, apparently just couldn't make a decision. So when the coup happened, I was still an active KGB officer.

Where were you on the night of August 18–19, 1991?*

I was on vacation. When it all started, I was really worried because I was way out in the sticks. I got back to Leningrad

---

*August 18–19, 1991, was the date of Russian president Boris Yeltsin's resistance to the attempted coup by Soviet hard-liners, which led to the breakup of the USSR in December 1991.

on the 20th. Sobchak and I practically moved into the city council. Well, not just us two—a whole bunch of people were camped out there, and we were there with them.

It was dangerous to drive out of the cty council compound, but we wanted to take some active measures. We drove to the Kirov Factory and to other plants to speak to the workers. But we were nervous. We even passed out pistols, although I left my service revolver in the safe.

People everywhere supported us. It was clear that if someone tried to disrupt the situation, there would be a huge number of casualties. But then that was it, the coup was over, and they chased away the coup-plotters.

What did you yourself think of them?

It was clear that they were destroying the country. In principle, their goal—preserving the Soviet Union from collapse—was noble, and they probably saw it that way. But the means and methods they chose only pushed the country further toward collapse. Once I saw the faces of the coup-plotters on TV, I knew right away that it was all over.

But let's say the coup had ended the way the plotters had planned. You're an officer of the KGB. You and Sobchak probably would have been tried.

But I was no longer a KGB officer. As soon as the coup began, I immediately decided whose side I was on. I knew for sure that I would never follow the coup-plotters' orders. I would never be on their side. I knew perfectly well that my behavior could be considered a crime of office. That's why, on August 20, I wrote a second statement resigning from the KGB.

But what if it had been blocked like your first letter?

I immediately warned Sobchak of that possibility. "Anatoly Aleksandrovich," I said. "I already wrote one letter, and it died somewhere. Now I have to write again." Sobchak immediately called Vladimir Kryuchkov [then KGB chief], and then he called the head of my KGB division. The next day, they informed me that my resignation memo had been signed. Kryuchkov was a true believer in Communism, who sided with the coup-plotters. But he was also a very decent man. To this day I have the greatest respect for him.

Did you suffer?

Terribly. In fact, it tore my life apart. Up until that time I didn't really understand the transformation that was going on in Russia. When I had come home from the GDR, it was clear to me that something was happening. But during the days of the coup, all the ideals, all the goals that I had had when I went to work for the KGB, collapsed.

Of course it was incredibly difficult to go through this. After all, most of my life had been devoted to work in the agencies. But I had made my choice.

Have you read the things that were published in *Moskovskiye Novosti* and *Ogonyok* in those days? For instance, General Kalugin's exposures? *

Oleg Kalugin served the KGB for 30 years, but eventually broke with the world of KGB secrecy, and, during the perestroika years under Mikhail Gorbachev, campaigned for public accountability among the security services. Kalugin was stripped of his many KGB decorations by KGB hard-liners in 1990. They were restored the following year.

Kalugin is a traitor. I saw Kalugin during my time in Leningrad when he was deputy head of the Directorate. He was an absolute loafer.

A loafer, perhaps, but he remembers you.
He doesn't remember anything.

He does remember, and he says that from the point of view of the intelligence service, you worked in a province and had nothing to show for your performance.
Oh, he doesn't remember a thing. He couldn't remember me. I had no contact with him, nor did I meet him. It is I who remembers him, because he was a big boss and everybody knew him. As to whether he knew me, there were hundreds of us.

Vladimir Churov:

A few months after the coup, the House of Political Enlightenment, which had belonged to the Communists, was given to the city. Fairly soon afterward an international business center was opened there. But the new leaders treated the Communists generously and left them part of the building. The Communist Party of the Russian Federation occupied almost a whole wing of the building, along with other Communist organizations. There was a flagpole on the roof of the building. The Communists decided to use it to hang a red flag. And each time the new city leaders drove out of Smolny, they would see that red flag. It was perfectly visible from the windows in Sobchak's and Putin's offices.

Putin gave the order to have the flag removed. But the next day it appeared again. Putin gave the order again—and again the flag was taken down. Back and forth it went. The Communists began to run out of flags and started using all sorts of things. One of their last versions wasn't even red but more of a dark brown. That put Putin over the edge. He found a crane, and under his personal supervision, had the flagpole cut down with a blowtorch.

When did you leave the Party?

I didn't. The CPSU ceased to exist. I took my Party card and put it away in a drawer.

How did St. Petersburg get through 1993?

It was just like Moscow, only people didn't shoot each other. The mayor's office was in the Smolny building by then, and the deputies were in the Leningrad City Council building.

So there was basically the same kind of conflict in Peter as Yeltsin had with the Supreme Soviet [parliament]?

Yes. But it is important to note that there wasn't the same division between the law-enforcement agencies that there had been in 1991. The FSB* leadership—Viktor Cherkesov was the head—announced their support for the mayor from the start. The FSB introduced a number of measures advocating the arrest of extremists who were plotting provocations, planning to blow things up, or trying to destabilize the situation. And that was the end of it.

Marina Yentaltseva (Putin's secretary from 1991 to 1996):

The first time I saw Vladimir Vladimirovich was from behind the glass door of an office. I was sitting across from the door and putting on my lipstick. Suddenly I saw the new director of the Committee for Foreign Liaison walking down the hall, and I thought, "Uh-oh, now he definitely won't hire me for the job." But everything was fine. He pretended that he hadn't noticed a thing, and I never put my lipstick on at work again.

---

*The FSB (Federalnaya sluzbha bezopasnosti) is Russia's Federal Security Service. It replaced the KGB. Putin was named director of the FSB in 1998.

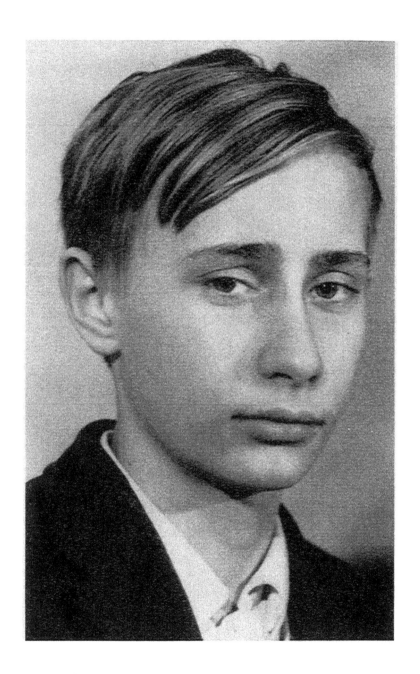

My mother
Mariya Ivanovna Shelomova

My father
Vladimir Spiridonovich Putin

Grandad was a cook
for Lenin and Stalin.

After he was wounded, my father worked on a collective farm.

My father in the navy in 1932.

With my mother in July, 1958

With my parents before I left for Germany in 1985

Grandma Olya lived her whole life in the country.

Sasha Grigoriev (right) runs the FSB in the St. Petersburg-Leningrad region.

Three photos of me in the KGB

My favorite portrait of Lyudmila.

I proposed to Lyudmila and three months later we married.
I married late in life, in 1983, when I was already thirty.

My first daughter, Masha, was born in 1985.

These are my lovely ladies.

At the dacha with our poodle Toska.

*Masha, on the right, wants to become a manager,
and Katya an interior designer.*

Judo is not just a sport. It's a philosophy.

Clinton is very charming.
(September 1999 in Aukland, New Zealand)

Boris Nicholayevich Yeltsin's birthday, February 1, 2000.

A few seconds later Boris Nicholayevich turned to me and said,
"Take care of Russia."

I wouldn't say that he was a strict boss. Only people's stupidity would make him lose his temper. But he never raised his voice. He could be strict and demanding and yet never raise his voice. If he gave an assignment, he didn't really care how it was done or who did it or what problems they had. It just had to get done, and that was that.

Vladimir Churov:

In 1991, Sobchak decided to create the Committee for Foreign Liaison at the Leningrad City Council. It was headed by Vladimir Putin.

At that time, the city's foreign trade was in the same shape as the whole country's. It was dominated by state monopolies and monstrous, government-authorized firms such as Lenfintorg or Lenvneshtorg. Customs, banking, investment, the stock market, and other such structures simply didn't exist.

The Committee had to quickly create the preconditions for cooperation with Western market economies. They began by opening the first branches of Western banks. With Putin's active involvement, they opened branches of Dresdner Bank and Banque Nationale de Paris.

The city administration concentrated on attracting foreign investors. The Committee created investment zones, such as the Parnas zone and the Pulkovo Heights zone, that still exist to this day. They also developed an original scheme: They invited a large investor, Coca-Cola, to take over a plot of land in Pulkovo Heights and install high-capacity power and communications cables, hoping that other companies would follow suit. It worked. After Coca-Cola developed their piece of land, Gillette came, then Wrigley, and then some pharmaceutical companies. An economic zone thus took shape within the city, where total investment now exceeds half a billion dollars.

Furthermore, with the Committee's encouragement, the city's infrastructure began to be modernized to create the conditions necessary for successful business. The first major deal that Putin supported was the completion of a fiber-optic cable to Copenhagen. This project had been initiated back in the Soviet era but never completed. Now the efforts were successful, providing St. Petersburg with world-class international telephone connections.

Finally, there was the problem of personnel. There were few specialists who spoke foreign languages. With Sobchak's support, Putin created a faculty of international relations at LGU. The first class was announced in 1994. Graduates of the program are now working in our Committee and in other organizations.

Much has been written in the St. Petersburg press about the food delivery scandal. What was that?

In 1992, there was a food crisis in the country, and Leningrad experienced big problems. Our businessmen presented us with a scheme: If they were allowed to sell goods—mainly raw materials—abroad, they would deliver food to Russia. We had no other options. So the Committee for Foreign Liaison, which I headed, agreed to their offer.

We obtained permission from the head of the government and signed the relevant contracts. The firms filled out all the necessary paperwork, obtained export licenses, and began exporting raw materials. The customs agency would not have let anything out of the country without the correct paperwork and accompanying documents. At the time, a lot of people were saying that they were exporting certain rare earth metals. Not a single gram of any metal was exported. Anything that needed special permission was not passed through customs.

The scheme began to work. However, some of the firms did not uphold the main condition of the contract—they didn't deliver food from abroad, or at least they didn't import full loads. They reneged on their commitments to the city.

A deputies' commission was created, headed by Marina Salye, who conducted a special investigation.

No, there wasn't any real investigation. How could there be? There was no criminal offense.

Then where does this whole corruption story come from?

I think that some of the deputies exploited this story in order to pressure Sobchak into firing me.

Why?

For being a former KGB agent. Although they probably had other motives too. Some of the deputies wanted to make money off those deals, and they wound up with nothing but a meddlesome KGB agent. They wanted to put their own man in the job.

I think the city didn't do everything it could have done. They should have worked more closely with law enforcement agencies. But it would have been pointless to take the exploiters to court—they would have dissolved immediately and stopped exporting goods. There was essentially nothing to charge them with. Do you remember those days? Front offices appeared all over the place. There were pyramid schemes. Remember the MMM company? We just hadn't expected things to get so far out of hand.

You have to understand: We weren't involved in trade. The Committee for Foreign Liaison did not trade in anything itself. It did not make purchases or sales. It was not a foreign trade organization.

But the granting of licenses?

We did not have the right to grant licenses. That's just it: A division of the Ministry for Foreign Economic Relations issued the licenses. They were a federal structure and had nothing to do with the municipal administration.

Sergei Roldugin:

Volodya changed a lot when he went to work at the mayor's office. We began to see less and less of each other. He was very busy. He would leave the house early and come back at night. And of course he was tired. Even when we grilled shish kebabs out at the dacha, he paced along the fence, lost in thought, in another place. He became wholeheartedly involved in St. Petersburg's affairs and then his emotions were drained. He had become a pragmatist.

Marina Yentaltseva:

The Putins had a dog, a Caucasian sheepdog called Malysh. The dog lived at the dacha and used to dig under the fence all the time and try to get outside. One day she did finally dig her way out, and she got hit by a car. Lyudmila Aleksandrovna scooped her up and took her to a veterinary clinic. She called from the vet's office and asked me to tell her husband that they weren't able to save the dog.

I went into Vladimir Vladimirovich's office and said, "You know . . . we have a situation . . . Malysh was killed." I looked at him, and there was zero emotion on his face. I was so surprised at the lack of any kind of reaction that I couldn't contain myself and said, "Did someone already tell you about it?" And he said calmly, "No, you're the first to tell me." And I knew I had made a blunder.

In fact, he is a very emotional man. But when he has to, he can hide his feelings. Although he also knows how to relax.

One night my friends and I went to an erotic show in Hamburg. Actually, it was hardly erotic. It was crude. And we were there with our wives! They were traveling abroad for the first time, and they had talked me into it. "Maybe it's better not to go?" I said. "No, no, we have to. We're grown-ups." "Well, alright," I said. "Remember that you're the ones who wanted to."

We went in, sat down at a table, and the show began. Some black performers came out on the stage—a huge black man, about two meters tall, and a black woman, who was just a little girl. Slowly they began to strip to some good music. Suddenly, without taking her eyes off the pair, my friend's wife got up from the table, stood, and then—*bang!*—fainted. It was a good thing her husband caught her, or she would have hit her head.

We revived her and took her into the bathroom, where we rinsed her face. We went up to the second floor and were walking around when the performers, who had just finished their number and come off the stage, passed by—stark naked. My friend's wife saw them and—*bang!*—she fainted again.

We sat down at the table. "How are you feeling?" I asked my friend's wife. Lowering her eyes, she replied, "I think it's something I ate. Everything's fine. It will pass." I said, "No, let's go. We've seen everything. We've gotten in touch with the sublime. Now let's scram."

Whenever there was a problem, I was there as a scout who knew the German language. It wasn't my first trip to Hamburg. You won't believe me, but I was assigned to study their red-light district as part of my job. At that time we were trying to bring order to the gambling business in St. Petersburg.

I don't know whether I was right, but I thought that the government should have a monopoly over the gambling business. My position contradicted the new Law on Anti-Monopoly Activity, but I still tried to do everything in my power so that the government could established strict control over the gaming industry.

We created a municipal enterprise that did not own any casinos but controlled 51 percent of the stock of the gaming businesses in the city. Various representatives of the basic oversight organizations—the FSB, the tax police, and the tax inspectorate—were assigned to supervise this enterprise. The idea was that the state, as a stockholder, would receive dividends from its 51 percent of the stock.

In fact, this was a mistake, because you can own tons of stock and still not really control something. All the money coming from the tables was cash and could be diverted. The casino owners showed us only losses on the books. While we were counting up the profits and deciding where to allocate the funds—to develop the city's businesses or support the social sector—they were laughing at us and showing us their losses. Ours was a classic mistake made by people encountering the free market for the first time.

Later, particularly during Anatoly Sobchak's 1996 election campaign, our political opponents tried to find something criminal in our actions and accuse us of corruption. They said the mayor's office was in the gambling business. It was almost comical to read this. Everything that we did was so absolutely transparent.

You can only argue about whether our actions were correct from an economic point of view. Obviously, the scheme was ineffective and we didn't achieve what we had planned. We hadn't thought things through sufficiently. But if I had remained in Peter, I would have squeezed those casinos to the end and forced them to work for the betterment of society and to share their profits with the city. That money would have gone to pensioners, teachers, and doctors.

Vladimir Churov:

We had an unpleasant incident when Vice President Al Gore visited our city. When the vice president was being met at the airport, an official of the U.S. Consulate General in St. Petersburg was rude to one of our city leaders. I don't remember exactly what happened, but I think the U.S. official pushed the district commander. After that incident, Vladimir Putin issued an official statement that we would refuse to deal with this U.S. official in the city admin-istration. The U.S. ambassador to Russia came to resolve the conflict. He even-tually recalled not only that official but the consul general as well. As a result, Putin had the greatest respect for the entire U.S. diplomatic corps.

Yet another international political clash took place, in Hamburg in March 1994. The president of Estonia, Lennart Meri, who incidentally was well acquainted with Putin and Sobchak, indulged in some crude attacks against Russia in a public speech at a seminar of the European Union. Putin and some other Russian diplomats were in the hall. After Meri made yet another deroga-tory remark, referring to Russians as "occupiers," Putin got up and walked out of the room. This was a brave act; the meeting took place in the Knights' Hall, with its 30-foot-high ceilings and smooth marble floor. As Putin exited, his footfalls echoed across the floor. To top it all off, the huge steel door slammed behind him with a resounding crash. As Putin later told it, he had tried to hold the door open, but it was too heavy. Our Foreign Ministry commended his action after the fact.

Marina Yentaltseva:

Vladimir Vladimirovich always seemed so calm when dealing with foreign delegations and people of very high rank. Usually when you talk to big bosses, you feel shy or uncomfortable. But Vladimir Vladimirovich was always at ease. I envied him and wondered how I could learn to be that way. So I was sur-prised when his wife told me that he was fairly shy by nature and that he had to work hard to seem at ease with people.

It was easy talking to him. Although at first glance he seems very serious, in fact it is easy to joke with him. For example, he would say, "Call Moscow and set up an appointment for a meeting at a specific time so that I don't have to sit in the waiting room and waste a hell of a lot of hours." And I would reply, "Yes, just like the people waiting in your front office." He would give me a mock-scolding look. "Marina!"

I had a good relationship with his wife, Lyudmila Aleksandrovna. She and I would talk just like good acquaintances. I remember one time when I was a guest in their home and we were sitting in the kitchen drinking tea. Vladimir Vladimirovich telephoned. She told him, "Marina and I are drinking tea." And he probably said, "Which Marina?" because his wife answered, "What do you mean, which Marina? Your Marina!"

We grew especially close after Lyudmila Aleksandrovna had the car accident.

In 1994, I was involved in negotiations with Ted Turner and Jane Fonda about holding the Goodwill Games in St. Petersburg. They had come in person, and I was accompanying them to all their meetings. They had a very tight schedule.

Suddenly I got a call from my secretary, telling me that Lyudmila had been in an accident. "Is it serious?" I asked. "No, apparently not. But the ambulance took her to the hospital just in case." "Let me try to get out of this meeting and go to the hospital," I said.

When I arrived at the emergency room, I spoke with the chief physician, who assured me, "Don't worry, she's not in any danger. We're just going to put a splint on, and everything will be fine." "Are you sure?" "Absolutely," he said. So I left.

Lyudmila Putina:

I was driving our Zhiguli and was going through a green light. Katya was asleep in the back seat. And suddenly another automobile came crashing into the side of our car. It was going about 80 kilometers an hour. I didn't even see it. I had the green light and didn't even look to the right. The other car had run a red light, swerving around another car that had stopped for the light.

We were fortunate that the driver crashed into the right front side of the car. If he had hit the front or back door, one of us would probably have been killed.

I lost consciousness for about half an hour, and when I woke up, I wanted to keep driving but I realized I couldn't. I hurt a little, and I was exhausted.

When the ambulance picked me up and gave me a sedative, I remember thinking, "Lord, now I'll catch up on my sleep!" I had not gotten enough sleep for several weeks.

My first thought, of course, was about my daughter. "What's happened to my child? My child was sitting in the back seat," I said immediately. And I gave one of the bystanders the telephone number of Volodya's assistant, Igor Ivanovich Sechin, so that he could come and pick Katya up, since the accident had taken place about three minutes away from Smolny. There was one bystander who was very concerned and helped me the most. She called the ambulance, she called Sechin, she took care of Katya, and she stayed nearby through the whole thing. Then she left her telephone number and it got lost somewhere in the car. That was too bad. I have wanted to thank her ever since.

The ambulance was summoned right away, but it took 45 minutes to get there. The doctors examined me and thought that my spine was broken. I was too timid to tell them to take me to the Military Medical Academy, to Yuri Leonidovich Shevchenko, so I was taken to another hospital, a place where people with traumas are always taken. The hospital was horrible. It was full of people who were dying. There were gurneys in the hallway with dead bodies on them. I'll remember it for the rest of my life. It was called the October 25th Hospital. If I had stayed there, I probably would have died, since they had no intention of operating on my spine. I don't think they even knew how.

Furthermore, they didn't even notice the fracture at the base of my skull. I would have suffered post-traumatic meningitis with a fatal outcome.

Marina Yentaltseva:

A woman called our office and said "Lyudmila Aleksandrovna asked me to call you. She's been in an accident. She asked me to telephone." What should I do in a situation like this? Vladimir Vladimirovich wasn't in his office. He was in the meeting with the foreigners. One of his deputies took a car, went to pick up Katya, and brought her right to the office in Smolny. I kept asking, "Katya, what happened?" And she said "I don't know. I was sleeping." She had been lying on the back seat. When the car crashed, she was probably thrown and knocked out.

At first I thought that Lyudmila Aleksandrovna was okay because she was in the doctors' care. And I needed to take the little girl to a doctor because she was bruised and seemed subdued. We went to a doctor right at Smolny, and he advised me to take her to a pediatrician.

We went to a children's neurologist at the pediatric institute to see if Katya had suffered a concussion. The doctor couldn't really tell us, but said that the child needed some peace and quiet. The doctor asked her what had happened, but Katya wasn't in any condition to explain anything. She was probably in shock.

The driver who had brought Katya to Smolny said that Lyudmila Aleksandrovna had been conscious when the ambulance came for her. I thought to myself, "Well, that's alright, then, it can't be too bad." Later I called the hospital to find out what the diagnosis was. Nobody told me anything about a skull fracture or a cracked vertebra.

Still, we were wondering. Vladimir Vladimirovich asked me to phone Yuri Leonidovich Shevchenko at the Military Medical Academy. He wasn't there. I phoned a second time, a third, a fourth, a fifth time, and he still wasn't there. Finally, late in the evening, I got a hold of him. And he immediately sent his surgeons over to remove Lyudmila Aleksandrovna from the hospital and bring her to his clinic.

So Dr. Shevchenko, the current Minister of Health, is someone you know well?

No, we didn't have a close relationship, even after my wife's accident. It's just that he's a real doctor. About four years ago, in 1996, during the first Chechen war, he removed a bullet from a soldier's heart. The bullet had plunged into the soldier's heart muscle, and the guy managed to stay alive. He flies to Peter on the weekends and does operations. He's a real doctor.

Lyudmila Putina:

Valery Yevgenevich Parfyonov brought me to the clinic. He saved my life by taking me out of the operating room. My ear was torn and they had decided to sew it up. They had left me naked on the table in a freezing operating room, in a terrible state of half-consciousness, and had gone away. When Valery Yevgenevich came, they told him, "She doesn't need anything. We just did an operation. Everything's fine."

He came into the operating room. I opened my eyes, and found an officer standing in front of me, holding my hand. He had a very warm palm. It warmed me up, and I knew that I had been saved.

They did an X ray at the Military Medical Academy and told me that I needed an emergency operation on my spine.

Marina Yentaltseva:

Lyudmila Aleksandrovna was staying with the children at the government dacha outside of town. Masha was still in school. When the accident happened, Lyudmila and Katya were on their way to pick her up. Katya was sick that morning and had not wanted to go anywhere, but she had asked to come along to pick up Masha.

Now I had to face picking up Masha and figuring out what to do with the children. I said to Vladimir Vladimirovich, "Let me take the girls out to my mother's house." He said, "No, that's awkward; but if you would agree to spend the night with the girls out at the dacha, I'd be very grateful." "Okay," I said.

On the way to the dacha we passed the second hospital where Lyudmila Aleksandrovna had been taken, and I saw Vladimir Vladimirovich's car. He was getting ready to leave. I asked the driver to pull over, and I got out of the car. "The girls are in the car," I told him. He went over to them, and I went into the hospital—they wouldn't allow the children in.

Lyudmila Aleksandrovna had just been operated on. She was conscious, and she asked me whether I had taken some warm clothing for the girls. It had gotten very cold that day, and there might not be warm things at the dacha.

When we were getting ready to leave, Vladimir Vladimirovich said that he would try to come back later but most likely wouldn't make it because his meetings would probably go late into the night.

The driver dropped us off at the dacha and left. But he forgot to tell us how to turn the heat on in the house, and it was terribly cold. The girls behaved beautifully. When we got to the house, they became helpful: "Aunt Marina, you have to take the blanket down from there, and the sheets are over here," they explained. They weren't in shock, and they didn't go weeping off into the corner. They tried to help.

The girls, of course, understood that it was all very serious. When we were on our way to the dacha and passed the hospital, and they saw their papa's car, they immediately asked "Is this where Mama is?" How did they know she had been taken to a new hospital? We hadn't told them about taking her to the Academy, so as not to worry them.

I put the girls in the same bed so they would be warm enough. At about three in the morning, I was startled by a knock on the door. I was frightened because there was no one else at the dacha. But it turned out that it was Vladimir Vladimirovich, who had at last gotten free from Ted Turner. He immediately found the switch and turned on the heater.

I had never seen him like this. I can't say that he was thrown for a loop and totally at a loss and didn't know what to grab on to. That wasn't the case. I just sensed that he was trying to come up with a plan in his head. Still, I never saw Vladimir Vladimirovich like this.

He came home at three in the morning, and left again at seven. I stayed with the girls until evening, when Ykaterina Tikhonovna, Lyudmila Aleksandrovna's mother, came from Kaliningrad.

How did she know?

I had sent her a telegram. Lyudmila Aleksandrovna might have been angry when she found out, but I did it anyway. I asked her to come—of course, with Vladimir Vladimirovich's consent. She stayed with the children until Lyudmila Aleksandrovna was released from the hospital.

Did she take a long time to recover?

She spent about a month and a half or even two months in the hospital. They also discovered a fracture at the base of her skull. That worried them much more than the crack in her spine.

Lyudmila Putina:

After the spinal operation, I lay in the intensive care unit and I kept telling the doctors that my jawbones were shifting around. And they kept joking, "Don't worry, we'll put in new ones." But then the surgeon who had operated on me decided to check it out, and just in case, to take an X ray. That's when they found the fracture at the base of my skull. They did another operation and began to treat me. I realize now that the doctors had great doubts about whether I was going to survive. I was lucky to make it out in one piece.

I only regret that they made incisions on both sides of my neck, front and back. Before the accident, it was a lot prettier.

Were you frightened at the diagnosis?

No, not particularly, because I was in intensive care, and delirious. I was just very sorry about my neck. I began to cry. When Valery Yevgenyevich, the surgeon, found out why I was crying, he said, "What a little fool! Her spine and skull are fractured, and she's crying because of some scars on her neck!"

I did cry. I was afraid those scars would be visible. In fact they turned out to be hardly noticeable.

Marina Yentaltseva:

She was in the hospital ward, in a room with four people, when she discovered the skull fracture herself. Vladimir Vladimirovich and the girls and I visited her all the time.

Lyudmila Putina:
When I got out of the hospital, I just crawled around my apartment for the first two weeks. Then, gradually, I began to be able to do things. In the end, it took me about two to three years to get back to my normal life.

Sergei Roldugin:
Once Volodya came to my dacha with his driver. We sat and talked for a while and then went to bed. And I noticed he put an air gun down next to him. Evidently something was amiss. I said, "Vovka, what are you doing? Do you think an air gun is going to save you?" "It won't save me," he said. "But it makes me feel calmer."

This happened in the last days of his job at the mayor's office, when Sobchak's electoral campaign was just getting off the ground.

From the outset, it was clear that the mayoral elections in 1996 would be very complicated for us. I warned Anatoly Aleksandrovich Sobchak that these elections were going to be hard.

In 1992, I had played a definitive role in Sobchak's election as the first popularly elected mayor of the city. As chair of the Leningrad City Council under the old system, Sobchak could have been removed by the council members at any moment. He needed a more stable position.

Sobchack finally agreed that we had to introduce the post of mayor. But because he had fairly conflictual relations with the majority of the deputies on the council, he wasn't sure that the proposition would pass. Meanwhile, his public popularity was very high. The deputies knew that Sobchak would be elected mayor if they voted to introduce the post. And they didn't want that. They liked the fact that they could always keep him on a hook.

Still, I was able to convince some of the deputies that it would be best for the city if we had the mayoral post. I also managed to mobilize the heads of the city districts. They didn't have the right to vote, but they could influence their deputies.

In the end, the decision to introduce the post of mayor was passed by the Leningrad City Council, by a margin of a single vote.*

Four years later it was clear that in order to win an election, he would need professional campaign managers and technicians—not just a guy who could finesse the deputies. This was a whole new ball game.

You gave Sobchak some advice on how he should run the campaign?

I told him right off, "You know, you're on a completely different playing field now. You need specialists." He agreed, but then he decided that he would conduct his own electoral campaign.

Out of overconfidence?

It's hard to say. You know, running a campaign, bringing in specialists—all of this costs money. And we didn't have any. Sobchak had been under investigation for a year and a half on allegations that he had bought an apartment with city funds. But in fact he didn't have any money either for an apartment or for an election campaign. We were not extracting funds from the city budget. It never even entered our heads to find the money we needed that way.

Yakovlev got the funds he needed—at Moscow's expense. He was supported by the very same people who orchestrated the campaign against Sobchak.

*The title for Sobchak was mayor, a new title introduced for the democratically-elected chair of the city council in the democratic reform period of the late 1980s and early 1990s. The name of the top leadership post in St. Petersburg was restored to governor in 1996 when Governor Yakolev was elected.

Korzhakov played an active role against him . . .

According to the information we had, Soskovets did, as well. The law-enforcement agencies were brought in later. They played very dirty.

About a year and a half before the elections, a commission came to St. Petersburg from Moscow. The commission had been appointed by the heads of three agencies: the FSB, the Interior Ministry, and the prosecutor's office. They opened up several criminal cases and made Sobchak a witness in two of them. During the election campaign, someone sent an inquiry to the Prosecutor General's office, asking whether Sobchak was involved in any criminal investigations. The very same day the answer came back: Yes, there were two criminal cases under investigation. Naturally, they didn't explain that he was a witness, not a suspect, in these cases. The reply from the Prosecutor General's office was duplicated, and flyers were dropped over the city from a helicopter. The law enforcement agencies were interfering directly in a political contest.

Sobchak decided to run his own campaign office. Lyudmila Borisovna, his wife, got involved, and he pronounced her campaign manager. We tried to talk both of them out of this, because we weren't convinced that everyone in the campaign office would be willing to take orders from her.

We lost a lot of time debating about who should run the campaign. Aleksei Kudrin, who was also a deputy of Sobchak's, got involved. But Sobchak asked me to continue to work in city affairs. Somebody had to manage the economic activity of a city with a population of five million citizens during that period. At the last minute, between the first and second rounds, Kudrin and I tried to jump into the fray, but by then it was hopeless. We really blew it on the election. For some time after our defeat in the mayoral elections, I stayed in my office in Smolny. The second round of the presidential elections was underway, and I was working for the St. Petersburg headquarters of Yeltsin's campaign. Vladimir Yakovlev, former governor of Leningrad oblast, now elected mayor of St. Petersburg, didn't kick me out of my office right away; but as soon as the presidential elections were over, I was asked rather harshly to free up the space. By that time I had already turned down Yakovlev's offer to keep my post as deputy mayor. He had made the offer through his people. I thought it would be impossible to work with Yakovlev, and I conveyed that to him.

Besides, during the campaign, I was the one who had initiated a statement signed by all the officials in the mayor's office that we would all leave Smolny if Sobchak lost. It was important to express our solidarity, so that all the people who worked with Anatoly Aleksandrovich and his administration would realize that his defeat would be a defeat for them, too. It was a good stimulus to get them all involved in the struggle.

We called a press conference and made a public statement, which I read. So it was impossible for me to remain behind in the mayor's office after Sobchak lost.

Furthermore, I had attacked Yakovlev during the election campaign. I don't remember the context now, but in a television interview I had called him a Judas. The word seemed to fit, and I used it.

Although my relations with Yakovlev didn't improve after that, oddly enough they also didn't deteriorate. Still, I couldn't stay behind with him. The same went for many of my colleagues. Misha Manevich came to me and said, "Listen, I want to get your advice. Yakovlev is offering me the job of vice mayor." I said, "Misha, of course you should take it." And he said to me, "How can I? We all agreed that we'd leave." I said to him, "Misha, what are you talking about? It was a campaign; we had to do that. But how can you leave all this? Who will work here? The city needs professionals." I talked him into staying.

Misha was an amazing guy. I am so sorry that he was murdered. It was such an injustice. Whose toes did he step on? It's just shocking. He was so mild, well mannered, and flexible in the best sense of the word. He had principles. He didn't accommodate everybody, but he never got on his high horse. He always looked for a way out, for an acceptable solution. I still don't understood how he could have been murdered. I just don't understand it.

Besides Misha, I talked several other colleagues into staying. Dima Kozak, who was head of the legal department, had already handed in his letter of resignation, and I talked him into coming back. But all told, a lot of people left Smolny.

Marina Yentaltseva:

I wrote my letter of resignation on the last day Vladimir Vladimirovich worked at Smolny. I left without having anywhere to go. There was no back up plan for me.

It had been hard working with Putin, but very interesting. It's always interesting, working with smart people. And I couldn't imagine ever working with anyone else. Vladimir Vladimirovich guessed my sentiments even before I handed in my resignation. He began to try to talk me out of it. "Marina, why have you decided to leave? Don't go," he said. He said that he didn't know where he was going to be working, and that he wasn't sure that he would be able to offer me a job in the future. I replied, "Regardless of whether you can offer me anything in the future or not, I still am not going to work here."

When I took my letter of resignation in for his signature, my eyes were wet. He noticed it, and tried to reassure me. "Marinochka, don't get so upset." I tried to get hold of myself. "Alright, that's it, I won't anymore." And he said, "Don't get so upset, please."

Of course I really suffered heavily through all this. I was sad to come to the end of such an interesting and quite meaningful period in my life. Still, I was absolutely certain that everything would work out fine for Vladimir Vladimirovich. I knew that such a smart person would not remain on the shelf for long.

In July, my family and I moved to the dacha that I had built several years earlier. I waited expectantly. Everyone was saying that I was "so needed by everybody" and that someone would definitely call me. Anatoly Sobchak had said he would definitely make me an ambassador. He had talked to Primakov. He told me, "I spoke to the minister. You'll be an ambassador." Of course I doubted that anyone would send me anywhere as an envoy, but it was awkward telling Sobchak the truth. I couldn't say "Anatoly Aleksandrovich, that's a total fantasy! You and I have no more hope of seeing an ambassadorship than we have of seeing our own ears!" And I was right.

Anatoly Aleksandrovich Sobchak was an emotional man. He liked to be the center of attention and to be talked about. It seemed to me that it didn't matter to him whether people were damning or praising him.

At the start of his job at the Leningrad City Council, Sobchak indulged in several sharp attacks on the army. He called the generals "blockheads," even though he didn't mean it, which I know for a fact. Sobchak had a positive attitude toward the army. But once when he was reaching for a snappy phrase in a public speech before a sympathetic audience, he used the word, and it was a mistake.

The generals really loathed him. Once there was a military meeting that he, as a member of the military council of the Leningrad Military District, was supposed to attend. It was on his calendar. But Alla Borisovna Pugacheva, the popular singer, was supposed to arrive in Leningrad at the same time. He said to me, "Listen, call the generals and tell them that I can't make it." He just wanted to meet Pugacheva. The generals had already moved their meeting once to accommodate his schedule. "You have to go," I told him. "Well, tell them I'm sick!" he said. And he went off to the airport to meet Pugacheva.

I called the commander, "You know, Anatoly Aleksandrovich is unable to come. He is sick." "Really? Alright, well, thanks for telling me." Two weeks later, I met the commander, and he said to me, insulted, "So he was sick, huh?" It turned out he had seen Sobchak meeting Pugacheva at the airport on television and that he had gone to her concert. And then he made an unkind remark about Lyudmila Borisovna, although she had nothing to do with it. "So he has time to meet with those . . . even when he's sick. And he has no time to be involved with government business?"

When Sobchak flew off to Paris, where were you?
In St. Petersburg, although I was already working in Moscow by then.

Tell us about it.
What's to tell?

Well, there was some convoluted story involving his departure. . . .
It wasn't convoluted. I was in Peter, so I went to visit him in the hospital.

You just went to say goodbye?
No, I didn't say goodbye. I just visited him in the hospital, and that was it. He was in the cardiac unit, and then Yura Shevchenko, the head of the Military Medical Academy, transferred him.

And then on November 7, his friends—I think they were from Finland—sent him a medevac plane, and he was flown to a hospital in France.

Just like that? Nobody organized anything in advance? Some people just sent an airplane?
Yes, his friends sent an airplane. Since it was November 7—a national holiday—his absence from St. Petersburg was not noticed until November 10.

From the outside, it all looked like a special operation organized by a professional.
What are you talking about? There was nothing special about it. The newspapers wrote that he was whisked out, without even going through customs. That's not true, he passed through customs and passport control at the border. Everything was as it was supposed to be. They put stamps in his passport. They put him on the airplane. That was that.

Applause, applause. But they could have arrested him?
They probably could have. But I don't know what for.

To this day you don't understand?
No, why are you saying that? In fact, I do understand that they had no grounds to arrest him. He had been implicated in this murky story of the apartment. A case was opened up, but

it fell apart in the end. They put the screws to Sobchak for four years and then hounded the poor guy all over Europe.

Did you yourself get to the bottom of this story?
No. Frankly, I didn't even know the details. Later, I looked into it for myself.

And did you find it interesting to dig into the details of this case because you wanted to know the kind of person you were working with? Or did you never have doubts at all?
You know, I was absolutely convinced that he was a decent person—100 percent decent—because I had dealt with him for many years. I know how he thinks, what he values, what he doesn't value, what he is capable of, and what he is incapable of.

Remember the episode in the film *The Sword and the Shield*, when the Germans are trying to recruit the Soviet officer? They say, "You think we'll let you die a hero? Here's a photo showing you in a German uniform. That's it, you're a traitor." The Soviet officer grabs a chair and tries to hit the recruiter. Then the recruiter shoots him and says, "It was the wrong idea from the start. There was no sense in blackmailing him. Obviously, that officer's reputation in his homeland is flawless."

The same is true of Sobchak. He is a decent man with a flawless reputation. Furthermore, he is very bright, open, and talented. Even though we are very different, I really like Anatoly Aleksandrovich. I really like people like him. He's real.

Few people know that Anatoly Aleksandrovich and I had very close, friendly, confidential conversations. We used to talk a lot, especially on our trips abroad, when we were left virtually alone for several days. He was a friend and mentor to me.*

Lyudmila Putina:
That summer of 1996, right after the elections, we moved out of the city to the house that we had been building for six years, about 100 kilometers outside of Petersburg. We lived there about six weeks. We sewed curtains, cleaned, settled in, and arranged the furniture. As soon as we had finished all this, the house burned down. It is a sad story. It burned to the ground.

Marina Yentaltseva:
We drove out to the Putins' dacha. They had just finished building it. We got there quite late, toward evening. My husband and I had wanted to go back the same day, but Vladimir Vladimirovich and Lyudmila Aleksandrovna started in: "What are you saying? Let's heat up the banya and have a steam bath!" And their daughters chimed in, "Let Svetulya stay!" Svetulya is our daughter.

Our house was made of brick, but finished with wood inside. On that day I was out at the dacha with my wife and kids. We had just moved in. Marina Yentaltseva, my secretary, had just arrived with her husband and daughter. We men went into the sauna, which is right inside the house on the first floor. We steamed ourselves for a while, then had a dip in the river and came back to the sauna rest room. Suddenly, I heard a crack. I saw some smoke, and then a flame came shooting out. In my loudest and most commanding voice, I yelled for everybody to get out of the house. The sauna was on fire.

Katya was in the kitchen, eating something. She turned out to be the most disciplined. When I shouted "Everybody get out of the house!" she dropped her spoon on the table and

This conversation took place two days before the tragic death of Anatoly Sobchak. On February 19, 2000, Sobchak died of a heart attack in the city of Svetlogorsk.—Authors

leapt out of the house without asking any questions. Then she stood outside the house and watched. I ran upstairs.

My older daughter, Masha, was another story. She was floundering around on the second floor. . . . I took Masha by the hand and brought her out to the balcony. Then I tore the sheets off the bed, knotted them together, tied them to the balcony railing, and said to Masha: "Climb down!" She got scared: "I'm not going, I'm afraid!" I threatened her: "I'm going to pick you up right away and throw you off here like a puppy! What's with you? Don't you understand that the house is about to burn down?!" I took her by the scruff of the neck and tossed her over the railing, and they caught her at the bottom.

Then I suddenly remembered there was a briefcase in our room with cash in it—all our savings. What would we do without that money? I went back and started looking, feeling around with my hand. I thought, well, I've got a few more seconds of this and then I won't be able to . . . I stopped looking for the stash. I ran out to the balcony. Flames were shooting upward. I clambered over the railing, grabbing the sheets, and began to lower myself down. And here's an interesting detail: I was stark naked from the banya. I had only just managed to wrap a sheet around myself. So you can imagine the scene: the house is burning, there's a naked man wrapped in a sheet, crawling down from the balcony, and the wind is blowing the sheet out like a sail. A crowd had gathered on the hill, and they were watching with enormous interest.

The two cars were parked next to the house, and they were heating up pretty rapidly. But the keys to them were inside the house, and the doors were locked.

Marina Yentaltseva:

We were left without keys. Everything was inside the house. Lyudmila Aleksandrovna said, "Let's push this one." We had a Model 9 Zhiguli. I shouted in hysterics, "To hell with the car! The house is on fire!" She looked at me with great surprise and said, "That's okay, we can still use it." She took a stone and threw it at the car window. Then she moved the gearshift out of "park," and we somehow managed to push the first car and then the other one.

Then I stood silently staring as the house burned. It was a total shock for me. Lyudmila Aleksandrovna was the first one to say, "Thank God, everyone is alive and well!"

The house burned like a candle. The firemen arrived, but they ran out of water right away. There was a lake right there. "What do you mean, you're out of water? There's a whole lake right here!" I said. "There's a lake," they agreed, "but no hose." The firemen came and went three times. Our dacha burned to the ground.

The girls suffered the most from this incident. They had brought all their treasures from home to the dacha—all their toys and Barbie dolls, which they had been accumulating their whole lives. Masha told me later that she couldn't sleep for several months after that. They had lost everything that was familiar to them.

When the firemen later analyzed the fire, they concluded that the sauna builders were to blame for everything—they hadn't put the stove in the banya properly. And if they were to blame, then they had to compensate us for the damage.

The first way they could compensate us would be to pay us money. But it wasn't clear how much the dacha was worth. The house burned down in 1996. We had been building it for five years. I remembered clearly that back in 1991, I had bought bricks for three rubles a piece. Later I realized that I didn't have enough and had to buy some more, but by then they cost seven rubles a piece. The prices since that time had risen further, and we had no idea how to index them.

So I liked the second option for compensation better—to force them to restore everything as it had been. And that's what they did. They erected the exact same frame, then hired a Polish firm to put on the finishing touches. They completed the job after a year and a half of work. Everything was as it had been before the fire, and even better. We only asked that the sauna be taken out completely.

Lyudmila Putina:

I was philosophical about the loss of the house. After that experience, I realized that houses, money, and things shouldn't add stress to your life. They aren't worth it. You know why? Because at any minute, they could all just burn up.

It's a national custom that all important matters are decided in the banya: What will you do now, without one?

Banyas are really just for bathing. Even that last time, we weren't trying to resolve any questions. We were just holding a wake for my former job.

Part 7

THE BUREAUCRAT

After a couple of false starts, Putin finally goes to Moscow in 1996. Government work suits him perfectly and he rises from post to post at dazzling speed. Then he is commanded to take over the FSB—the former KGB. This comes as a blow. Putin and Lyudmila do not want to return to the closed, stifling, stressful life of the secret services. Putin refuses the rank of general, becoming the first-ever civilian director of a security organ. Thankfully, the post doesn't last very long. Out of the blue, Yeltsin names Putin prime minister. Meanwhile, tension in the Caucuses is rising as Chechen rebels demand independence. Fearing a potential domino effect, Putin takes a hard line. He is willing to sacrifice his own political career to crush the Chechens and thereby avoid what he sees as a devastating, large-scale war.

What did you do for work after leaving Yakovlev's office, when no ambassadorial post materialized?

After we lost the elections in Peter, a few months passed and I was still without a job. It really wasn't very good. I had a family, you know. The situation had to be resolved, one way or another. But the signals from Moscow were mixed; first they were asking me to come to work, and then they weren't.

But who did make you an offer?

Borodin, as odd as it may seem.

Chief of Staff Pavel Borodin brought me into the presidential administration. I don't know why. We had met several times. That was essentially the extent of our relationship. Borodin talked to the chief of the presidential administration, Nikolai Yegorov, about me. Yegorov summoned me to Moscow and offered me a job as his deputy. He showed me a draft presidential decree and said that he would take it to Yeltsin's office for a signature next week and I could start work. I agreed, saying "Good. What am I supposed to do?" He said, "Fly home to Peter. When he signs it, we'll call you."

I left, and two or three days later Yegorov was removed from his post and Anatoly Chubais was made chief of administration. Then Chubais eliminated the job that had just been offered to me. So I ended up not moving to Moscow.

Some time passed, and there was another change of administration, now under Chernomyrdin. Aleksei Alekseyevich Bolshakov was his first deputy. He was a fellow-Petersburger. Bolshakov ran into Borodin at a reception, and said to him, "What are you doing? You promised the guy a job and then you dropped him, and now he's sitting there without a job." Borodin was insulted. "I didn't drop him. It was our little pal Chubais who ruined it." "Then take him on at your office," Bolshakov said. But Borodin thought I wouldn't go to the General Department because I had grown accustomed to other kinds of work. Bolshakov insisted: "Well, then think up something else." On that note, they parted, and Borodin promised to think of something. And so he did, but I only found out about it later.

Aleksei Kudrin called me. At that time he was chief of the president's Main Control Directorate.* He told me to come over and they'd see what they could do. Although the one post had been eliminated, there were other possibilities. I flew to Moscow and met with Kudrin, and he talked to Chubais. Chubais, before leaving to go on vacation, offered me a job heading the Directorate for Public Liaison. That really wasn't my cup of tea, but what could I do? If I had to work with the public, then I would work with the public. The job would still be in the president's administration. So I agreed to take it.

Kudrin and I got into his car and took off for the airport. On the way he said, "Listen, let's call up Bolshakov and con-

*The U.S. equivalent of Russia's Main Control Directorate is the Inspector General's Office.

gratulate him. He's one of us, from Peter, and he's been promoted to first deputy." "Well, alright," I said. We dialed Bolshakov's phone number right from the car and were
transferred through to him. As head of the Main Control
Directorate, Kudrin could get through to anyone. Aleksei
congratulated Bolshakov, and added, "Here's Volodya Putin,
and he'd like to congratulate you as well." Bolshakov said,
"Put him on the phone." I took the phone, and Bolshakov
said, "Where are you?" using the familiar form of address.
"What do you mean, I'm right here in the car. I'm going with
Aleksei to the airport." "And where were you?" he said. "At
the Kremlin. They were deciding which job I should have. I'm
going to be the head of the Directorate for Public Liaison."
"Call me back in 30 minutes," said Bolshakov. But the car
was getting closer to the airport.

I was all ready to board my plane, when at the last minute
Bolshakov called us back. "Listen, can you stay in Moscow?"
he asked. "I'll go see Borodin tomorrow." I didn't understand
what he was talking about, but I stayed. It never occurred to
me that Bolshakov remembered me. I didn't know why he
was doing this, but I didn't feel comfortable asking him.

I could think of only one explanation. You see, Aleksei
Alekseyevich Bolshakov was a prominent person. At one
time, he was the first deputy of the executive committee of
the Leningrad City Council, the person who really ran the
city. There were good reports about Bolshakov—that he was
a can-do, energetic, hard working man. Though he had never
really been an orthodox Communist, the tide of democracy
had swept him away. Sobchak decided that he had to go.

Bolshakov wound up almost on the street. He got some
work, but no one imagined that he would land himself a good
post again, much less in Moscow. From time to time, Bol-

shakov would appear in Smolny on business. I never forced him to wait in the reception area. I would always stop what I was doing, kick everybody out, come out into the reception area myself, and say, "Aleksei Alekseyevich, right this way." We were never close, but maybe he remembered me.

The next morning, I went to Borodin, and he offered me a job as his deputy.

That is how, in August 1996, I ended up in the government building on Old Square in Moscow, as deputy to the head of the president's General Affairs Department. I was in charge of the legal division and Russian property abroad.

Lyudmila Putina:

It wasn't a question of whether or not to go to Moscow. It was understood that we had to go. And I wouldn't even say that Volodya and I discussed his new appointment very much. Volodya said that although they had offered him a new job that wasn't quite suitable for him, there were no other options. Then he got the other offer.

I didn't want to leave St. Petersburg. We had just started living in our own apartment, and now everything was going to be government-issue again. But how could I complain? We got a dacha in Arkhangelsk. True, the house was old, but it had two floors and six rooms—two below, and four on the second floor—fancy! And I fell in love with Moscow right away. The city just suited me. Maybe it was the atmosphere, or the bustling streets, or the fact that it's well kept. I was wild about Petersburg, but when I came to Moscow I got over it. My husband took longer to get used to Moscow, but he also grew accustomed to it. Here, you really get the feeling that life is in full swing.

I wouldn't say that I didn't like Moscow. It's just that I liked Peter more. But Moscow is a truly European city. It has its problems, of course, but life is bustling. I have to admit that Peter is provincial, at least politically.

You have had an incredible career in Moscow. You got a promotion practically every year. In 1997, head of the Main Control Directorate; in 1998, first deputy head of the presidential administration, responsible for the regions; in 1998, director of the FSB, and later, secretary of the security council. In August 1999, prime minister, and since December 31, acting president. Have all of these positions held equal interest for you?

Not at all. In fact, there was a moment when I thought about leaving the presidential administration.

When was that?

When I worked in the Control Directorate. It was not very creative work. It was important, it was necessary, and I understood all that. But it simply wasn't interesting for me. I don't know what I would have done if I had left. I probably would have opened up a law firm. It's hard to say whether I could have lived on that, but it would have been interesting. Many of my friends are in private practice, and it's working out for them.

So why didn't you leave?

While I was still thinking about it, I was appointed first deputy to the chief of the presidential administration, responsible for the regions and contacts with the governors. To this day I think that was the most interesting job. I developed relationships with many of the governors at that time. It was clear to me that work with the regional leaders was one of the most important lines of work in the country. Everyone was saying that the *vertikal*, the vertical chain of government, had been destroyed and that it had to be restored.

But do the governors themselves need that? Are they ready to line up under the *vertikal*?

They are. After all, the governors are part of the country, and they also suffer from management weaknesses. Not everyone is going to like everything. You can't please everybody, but you can find some common approaches. I was also interested in learning more about the country. I had only ever worked in St. Petersburg, apart from the time I spent abroad. . . . Of course, my seven years of experience in Peter was good experience, both administrative and managerial. But Peter isn't the whole country. I wanted to travel and see things.

So, why did you drop that interesting job and go to work as director of the FSB? Do you have some affinity for the agencies?

No. I wasn't asked whether or not I wanted to go, and they had given me no inkling that I was even being considered for such an appointment. The president simply signed a decree. . . .

But the chief of administration was Valentin Yumashev?

Yes. I was sitting in my office, when the phone rang. "Can you get out to the airport and meet Kirienko?" Kirienko was prime minister, and he was coming back from a visit with the president, who was on vacation in Karelia. I said, "Alright." What was this all about, I wondered. I was already suspecting something bad. I got to the airport and Kirienko came out. He said, "Hi, Volodya! Congratulations!" I said, "What for?" He said, "The decree is signed. You have been appointed director of the FSB." Well, thanks a lot, guys. . . . I can't say I was overjoyed. I didn't want to step into the same river twice.

You know, working in a military-style organization is, after all, a very difficult kind of service. I remember coming into the KGB building where I worked and feeling as if they were plugging me into an electrical outlet. I don't know, maybe I was the only one who felt that way, but I think the majority of people who worked there did too. It put you in a constant state of tension. All the papers are secret. This isn't allowed, that isn't allowed.

And you couldn't even go out to a restaurant! They thought only prostitutes and black-marketeers went to restaurants. What would a decent officer of the security agencies be doing in such company?

And then, if you were an intelligence officer, you were always the object of a potential vetting. They are always checking up on you. It might not happen very often, but it wasn't very pleasant. And the meetings every week! And the plan of work for the day! You shouldn't laugh. There was a notebook stamped "Classified," and on Friday you had to come in, open it up, and write your work plan for the week— day by day. And then each day, you signed off on every hour.

In the Kremlin, I have a different position. Nobody controls me here. I control everybody else. But at the FSB I reported to the division head and the department head. He would open the work plan: What had been done during the week? And I would begin to report, and explain why something wasn't finished. I would explain that something was a large-scale project and that it couldn't be finished immediately. Then why did you put it in the plan? Only write down what you can do!

I'm telling you all this to explain what it was like. There was a lot of pressure.

I went into the office of the FSB director, and I was met by my predecessor, Nikolai Kovalev. He opened the safe and said, "Here's my secret notebook. And here's my ammunition." And I looked at all this mournfully.

Lyudmila Putina:

I believe the only appointment that we discussed at home was Volodya's post of prime minister. I remember we talked about the FSB once, about three months before he was offered the post, and he said that he would never agree to take it. We were taking a walk at the dacha in Arkhangelsk and talking about his work, and he said that he did not want to go to the FSB. I understood why. It would mean a return to the closed life. When Volodya worked in the KGB, it was really a very closed life. Don't go there, don't say that. Talk to that person, don't talk to this person. And then it had been such a hard decision to leave the KGB, that when he left, he thought he was leaving forever.

I was vacationing on the Baltic Sea when he called and said, "You be careful there, because I've been returned to the place where I began." I thought that he had given back the job as Borodin's deputy—that he had been demoted. I couldn't decode what he was saying. I thought that something had happened in the country while I was away, that the situation had changed somehow. Then he repeated it: "I've been returned to the place where I began." And when he said it the third time, I got it. When I got back from vacation, I asked him how it had happened. "They appointed me, and that's it." I asked no more questions.

When Volodya returned to the FSB, they offered him the rank of general. He was still in the civil service. But you can't have a colonel commanding generals. You need someone with authority.

Did this new position affect our lives? No, but I had some friends in Germany—a husband and wife—and I was forced to break off all contact with them. I thought it would just be for a while, but to this day, we have not renewed our friendship.

How did they greet you at the FSB? There you were, a former KGB colonel . . .

I was greeted cautiously. Then things got better. As for being a colonel . . . Let's take a closer look. . . . . First of all, I was a colonel in the reserves. I had completed my service as a lieutenant colonel, ten years earlier. During those ten years, I had had a different life. And when I came to work at the FSB, it was not as a colonel but as a civilian who held the position of first deputy to the chief of the presidential administration.

That is, you in fact became the first civilian leader of the security agencies?

Of course, but nobody paid attention to that, either because they were stupid or ignorant, or because they didn't want to.

Did the top leadership change under you?

It changed, but not a lot. I didn't make any drastic moves, really. I just took a look at the situation and the people and began to make the changes that I felt were necessary.

Why did Yevgeny Primakov say that you had put Leningraders everywhere?

Others said that I had fired all the Leningraders and put in unknowns. But I took the whole FSB leadership to Primakov for a meeting. And it turned out that everybody was in place. Nobody had been fired. Primakov then apologized, and said that he had been misled.

Is it true that as director of the FSB, you used to run into Vladimir Kryuchkov?*

It's true.

---

*Vladimir Kryuchkov was the former head of the KGB, and was one of the August 1991 coup-plotters.

Accidentally?

No, not accidentally. I worked rather actively with the longtime veterans.

People have started to talk again about merging the FSB with the MVD, the Interior Ministry. What do you think about this?*

I'm against it. The community of special services has coalesced, and to disrupt it again would be bad. From the perspective of ministerial concerns, it might be okay; but from a policy perspective, it would not be advantageous—it is better to receive information from two sources than from one.

So maybe it would be even better if they kept watch over each other rather than merging their forces?

That's not a question for me. In Germany, of course, it was like that in 1933. Everybody was supposed to watch over everybody else. That was the principle behind the Gestapo.

It's interesting to note that you were twice appointed to posts previously occupied by another Petersburger, Sergei Stepashin. First, with the FSB, which was then called the FSK; and later the post of prime minister. Is Stepashin not remembered fondly at the FSB?**

No, just the opposite, he was well liked. In the FSK, he handled himself in an unexpectedly mature manner, which earned many people's respect, including my own.

---

*On March 6, 1953, the day after Stalin died, his secret police chief, Lavrenty Beria, succeeded in merging the MVD with the MGB, as the KGB was then known. The merger lasted about a year, until Beria's execution in March 1954.

**The FSK was the Federal Counterintelligence Service.

Sobchak very much supported Stepashin's appointment as head of the Leningrad directorate of the FSK. I was already working in the city administration by that time. I recall Sobchak telling me that after the coup, a democrat was going to head the FSK. I didn't like that at all. Here . . . some kind of policeman was going to be running the agencies. In the *Cheka*,* we've never liked policemen. Besides, Stepashin never had any relationship to the security agencies. No, I honestly wasn't bothered by the fact he represented the democratic wave. I myself was already from that milieu. But I was surprised. Do you remember the situation of the security agencies at that time? People wanted to tear them down, to break them apart, to shred them to bits. They proposed opening up the lists of agents and declassifying files. But Stepashin behaved completely unexpectedly. In fact, he used his democratic authority to protect the Leningrad special services. From the outset he said, "If you trust me, then trust me. What we can publicize, we will. But what will be harmful to the state, we won't publicize." You have to give him credit; he was able to establish working relationships with the leaders of the agencies. He was trusted.

Later, Stepashin and I met in Moscow. We were not very close or friendly. But do you remember that after he resigned from the FSK, he worked in the government bureaucracy? I was in the presidential administration by then. And when the question arose of whom to appoint as Minister of Justice, I suggested Stepashin. I had discussed it with him beforehand: "Sergei, do you want it? I don't know if I'll be able to put it

---

*Cheka, *a word formed from the Russian acronym for "Extraordinary Commission," is the name of the secret police organization founded by Lenin. The word is still popularly used to refer to the security police.*

through, but I'm prepared to support you," I said. He said he did want it, because he was tired of pushing papers.

Were you happy when Stepashin was appointed prime minister?
Yes.

And did you know that at the same time, you were being considered as a candidate for this post?
When he was appointed premier? No. No, it never entered my mind.

Stepashin served as prime minister for only a few months. He didn't hide the fact that his dismissal was very painful for him. Did you speak to him face-to-face?
Yes. He knows I had nothing to do with his dismissal. Still, it was terribly awkward when I was telephoned on the eve of the event and asked to come to visit Yeltsin at The Hills the next morning. The four of us were sitting there together— Boris Nikolayevich Yeltsin, Stepashin, Nikolai Aksenenko, and I—when Yeltsin demanded Sergei's resignation. You can imagine the state I was in. I am his colleague! What was I supposed to say—Sergei, you're going to be fired? I couldn't say that aloud. I wouldn't be able to get the words out. Of course, it was all very unpleasant.

After you left Yeltsin's, did you talk to each other?
We said goodbye, and that was it.

And you and Stepashin never spoke about that morning again?
We did talk about it. I think he was offended. Or he was hurt. Time will pass, and he'll forget about it. He hadn't done

anything obvious for which he deserved to be fired. But the president believed otherwise. He made the decision, and it probably wasn't just based on the two or three months that Sergei was prime minister. . . .

Boris Nikolayevich invited me to his office and said that he was thinking about offering me the post of prime minister but that he had to talk to Stepashin first. I wasn't especially surprised. It was clear that things were moving in that direction. I mean, not my appointment, but Stepashin's dismissal. Yeltsin didn't ask me if I would agree to become prime minister or not. He just said that he had already made a decision regarding Stepashin.

By the way, in his conversation with me, Yeltsin didn't use the word "successor." He used the phrase "prime minister with a future"—that is, if everything went smoothly, it was a possibility.*

And then later, on television, Yeltsin mentioned me as a possible future president. He said this aloud to the whole country. And when I was deluged with questions, I replied, "If the president says so, that's what I'll do." Maybe I didn't sound so sure of myself, but what else could I say?

Do you remember the state the country was in at the time? It was right before the elections, and Boris Nikolayevich had to make a decision. All those governors we've been talking about understood perfectly well that everything was frozen and that they had to make up their minds. Why did they form

---

Yeltsin changed prime ministers four times in 1989–1999. The order of Yeltsin's prime ministers is: Viktor S. Chernomyrdin (December 1992–March 1998), Sergei V. Kiriyenko (five months), Yevgeny M. Primakov (eight months), Sergei V. Stepashin (three months), Vladimir Putin (since August 10, 1999).

the OVR?* Because the governors had no alternative. They had to create an alternative.

You mean an alternative to Unity?*
Yes.

Lyudmila Putina:

I wasn't surprised that my husband's career advanced at the speed of lightning. But sometimes I would catch myself thinking: "How strange; I'm married to a man who yesterday was really just an unknown deputy mayor of St. Petersburg, and now he's the prime minister." But somehow I always believed that this could happen to Volodya.

I'm not afraid of it. And I'm not particularly proud. But I do admire Volodya. He's dedicated—not vain, but dedicated. He always worked hard and achieved his goals. He always lived for the sake of something. There are some people who work hard for money, but he works hard for ideas. He's satisfied by the very process of work. It seems to me that people like that go far. You know, the fact that I am the prime minister's wife is more surprising to me than that he is the prime minister.

Marina Yentaltseva:

A few days after Putin became prime minister, his father died. Every weekend Vladimir Vladimirovich had been coming from Moscow to visit his father. At that time he was very burdened with work, but he would still come to St. Petersburg once a week, for at least half a day. He was afraid that he wouldn't get there in time to say goodbye to his father. But I was told that he was present for the last few hours of his father's life.

*The OVR is the Fatherland–All Russia Party.

**Unity is Putin's party, created in December 1999.

When Yeltsin announced to the whole country that you were his successor, were you quaking inside?
No.

You were so sure of yourself?
No, that's not it. Remember what Gennady Seleznev said at the time: "Why did they do that to you? They've buried you." Everybody thought that that was the end for me. I also realized my career could be over, but for different reasons.

Let me try to explain. All of this took place as tension was mounting in Dagestan. I had already decided that my career might be over, but that my mission, my historical mission—and this will sound lofty, but it's true—consisted of resolving the situation in the Northern Caucasus. At that time nobody knew how it would all end; but it was clear to me—and probably to other people too—that "the kid was going to get his butt kicked" on the Northern Caucasus. That's how I saw it. I said to myself, "Never mind, I have a little time—two, three, maybe four months—to bang the hell out of those bandits. Then they can get rid of me."

I realized we needed to strike the rebel bases in Chechnya. Frankly, everything that had been done in recent years, especially in the area of preserving the government, was—how can I put it mildly, so as not to offend anyone?—amateurish. . . . Believe me, back in 1990–1991, I knew exactly—as arrogant as it may sound—that the attitude toward the army and the special services, especially after the fall of the USSR, threatened the country. We would very soon be on the verge of collapse. Now, about the Caucasus: What's the situation in the Northern Caucasus and in Chechnya today? It's a continuation of the collapse of the USSR. Clearly, at some point it has to be stopped. Yes, for a time, I had hoped that the growth of the economy and the emergence of democratic institutions would help freeze this process. But time and experience have shown us that this isn't happening.

This is what I thought of the situation in August, when the bandits attacked Dagestan: If we don't put an immediate end to this, Russia will cease to exist. It was a question of preventing the collapse of the country. I realized I could only do this at the cost of my political career. It was a minimal cost, and I was prepared to pay up. So when Yeltsin declared me his successor and everyone thought that it was the beginning of the end for me, I felt completely calm. The hell with them. I calculated that I had several months to consolidate the armed forces, the Interior Ministry, and the FSB, and to rally public support. Would there be enough time? That's all I worried about.

But the decision to begin a campaign in Dagestan and then in Chechnya wasn't yours to make. Yeltsin was president, and the burden of the first unsuccessful operation lay with him and with Stepashin.

Well, Stepashin was no longer prime minister. As for Yeltsin, he supported me completely. We discussed the situation in Chechnya at every meeting.

So that means that the entire responsibility was on your shoulders?

To a large degree. I met with the top officials of the Ministry of Defense, the General Staff, and the Interior Ministry. We met almost every day—sometimes twice a day, morning and evening. And with a lot of fine-tuning, the ministries were consolidated. The first thing that I had to do was overcome the disarray among the ministries. The army didn't understand what the Interior Ministry was doing, and the FSB was criticizing everyone and not taking responsibility for anything. We had to become one team, one single organism. Only then would we be successful.

You talked about the price that you personally were prepared to pay for the campaign in the Northern Caucasus: your career. But in fact, the price of any military campaign is measured in human lives and in units of currency.

I was convinced that if we didn't stop the extremists right away, we'd be facing a second Yugoslavia on the entire territory of the Russian Federation—the Yugoslavization of Russia.

But you could have knocked the rebels out of Dagestan, and surrounded Chechnya with a cordon sanitaire . . .

That would have been pointless and also technically impossible.

Tell us, does the fact that Lenin gave Finland away many decades ago bother you? Is the secession of Chechnya impossible in principle?

No, it isn't. But secession isn't the issue.

It seemed to me that it was all absolutely clear. I'll tell you what guided me and why I was so convinced of the threat that hung over our country. Everyone says I'm harsh, even brutal. These are unpleasant epithets. But I have never for a second believed—and people with even an elementary level of political knowledge understand this—that Chechnya would limit itself to its own independence. It would become a beach-head for further attacks on Russia.

After all, the aggression began there. They built up their forces and then attacked a neighboring territory. Why? In order to defend the independence of Chechnya? Of course not. In order to seize additional territories. They would have swallowed up Dagestan, and that would have been the begin-ning of the end. The entire Caucasus would have followed—Dagestan, Ingushetia, and then up along the Volga River to Bashkortostan and Tatarstan, reaching deep into the country.

You know, I was frightened when I imagined the real con-sequences. I started wondering how many refugees Europe and America could absorb. Because the disintegration of such an enormous country would have been a global catastrophe. And when I compare the scale of the possible tragedy to what we have there now, I do not have a second of doubt that we are doing the right thing. Maybe we should be even tougher. The problem is, if the conflict goes further, no amount of armed forces will be enough. We would be forced to draft people in the reserves and send them into combat. A large-scale war would begin.

Another option: We could agree to a division of the coun-try. Immediately, dissatisfied leaders from different regions and territories would turn up: "We don't want to live in a Russia like that. We want to be independent." And off they'd go.

Now, let's return to the question of the independence of Chechnya. Today, everyone recognizes that it is necessary to preserve the territorial integrity of Russia and not to support terrorists and separatists. But let's say we agreed to the inde-pendence of the republic and allowed Chechnya to succeed.

The situation would be completely different. If we agreed to Chechnya's independence, then quite a few countries would immediately grant official recognition to Chechnya, and that very same day, would begin to provide large-scale official support to the Chechens. Our current actions would be viewed as aggression, and not the resolution of internal problems. This would radically change the situation and make it far, far worse for Russia.

Last summer, we began a battle—not against the independence of Chechnya but against the aggressive aspirations that had begun to flourish on that territory. We are not attacking. We are defending ourselves. We knocked the rebels out of Dagestan, and they came back. We knocked them out again, and they came back again. We knocked them out a third time. And then, when we gave them a serious kick in the teeth, they blew up apartment houses in Moscow, Buinaksk, and Volgodonsk.

Did you make the decision to continue the operation in Chechnya before the apartment house explosions or after?
    After.

You know that there is a version of the story that says the apartment houses were deliberately blown up, in order to justify the beginning of military actions in Chechnya? That is, the explosions were supposedly the work of the Russian special services?
    What?! Blowing up our own apartment buildings? You know, that is really . . . utter nonsense! It's totally insane.
    No one in the Russian special services would be capable of such a crime against his own people. The very supposition is

amoral. It's nothing but part of the information war against Russia.

Lyudmila Putina:

About three weeks before New Year's Eve, Volodya said, "I'm flying to Chechnya for New Year's. Are you coming with me?" At first I was surprised. How could I leave the children alone? And what if something happened to both of us: What would happen to them? I decided I wouldn't go. A few days later I flew to Peter, thought calmly for awhile, returned to Moscow, and told Volodya that I would go to Chechnya after all. I don't know why. . . . I think I was terrified of staying behind without him. No one could guarantee that something wouldn't happen. Things were unpredictable.

The wife of Patrushev, director of the FSB, also came along. The rest were all men. We flew to Makhachkala, the capital of Dagestan, then transferred to three helicopters and flew to Gudermes, the second largest city of Chechnya. But the pilot decided not to risk landing the helicopter in Gudermes—the visibility was poor. I think he needed to see ahead at least 150 meters, but he could only see 100. Twenty minutes before the New Year, we turned around and flew back. At midnight we opened champagne in the helicopter. We had no glasses, so we drank right out of the bottles. There were two bottles of champagne for the entire group.

When we turned back, the people in Gudermes figured that we weren't going to make it. But you have to know Volodya. I didn't have a minute's doubt that we would somehow reach that military unit. It wasn't important when or how, but we would get there. When we got back to Makhachkala, Volodya said to me, "You stay behind. We'll go in cars." No way! Was it worth flying such a long way to sit and wait for who knows how long? We piled into some cars. It was already 2:30 A.M. Two and a half hours later, we arrived at the unit. I slept the whole way.

You should have seen the surprise and amazement in the eyes of our boys when we arrived. They looked tired and a little disoriented—as though they wanted to pinch themselves: Was this really Putin who had come to see them and celebrate New Year's Eve with them? Were they dreaming?

We spent an hour in the unit and then drove back. Several hours later, the road on which we had just been traveling was bombed. That was it. Then we flew back to Moscow. On January 1, we were invited to the home of Boris Nikolayevich Yeltsin. It was only the second time in my life that I saw him.

Masha:

We kept asking our parents, "Where will we spend New Year's Eve?" And about a week before the holiday, Mama said that she and Papa would be away for New Year's. But she didn't say where they were going. My sister and I didn't think about it much. We weren't hurt that they were going away. Our aunt and cousin were visiting, and we had invited a girlfriend over. We had already received our presents. We had asked for a computer, and they had given us two, so that we each had our own. Our parents came back the next evening and went out again right away. It was only later, watching television, that we realized they had been in Chechnya.

Part 8

THE FAMILY MAN: INTERVIEW WITH LYUDMILA PUTINA

Interviews with Putin, Lyudmila, and their two daughters, Masha and Katya, take us inside the Putin home. Of course, things have changed since Papa's rise to power, but the family tries to remain clearheaded about their newly found fame. They share their shopping habits, TV preferences, and talk frankly about their father's temper and the pressures of being the First Family.

You've lived with your husband for 20 years. You must know everything about him.

No, you can never know everything about a person. Something remains secret in every person.

He's not very talkative?

I wouldn't call Volodya the silent type. He's very eager to talk about topics that interest him, with people who interest him. But he is not inclined to discuss people, especially the people he works with. I'm just the opposite. If I know someone or I see someone on television, I tend to express my opinion. And he doesn't like to do that.

Well, express yourself about somebody. What about Chubais, for instance. Do you know him?

A little bit.

Women usually like him.

And it seems to me that he doesn't take women seriously. He treats them with a certain contempt. I'm not a feminist, but I want women to occupy the place they deserve in this world.

Do you influence your husband? He's always saying that Russian women are underestimated.
That's hardly my influence. Our views just coincide.

Does he ever look at women?
I think that beautiful women attract his attention.

Do you take that calmly?
Well, what sort of man would he be, if he weren't attracted by beautiful women?

A lot of husbands bring their work frustrations home with them at the end of the day.
Volodya has never taken his problems out on me. Never! He has always solved them himself. Also, he won't discuss a problem until he has found a solution himself. Later he might say something. But I always sense when he has some problems or when he's simply in a bad mood. That's something he's not able to hide. In general he's a composed person, but at certain moments it's better not to bother him.

Or else there will be a fight?
It depends on what you mean. If you mean breaking dishes and flinging saucepans, no. He doesn't even raise his voice. But he can answer rather sharply.

Can he get drunk?
There hasn't been any of that. He is indifferent to alcohol, really. In Germany, he loved to drink beer. But usually he'll drink a little vodka or some cognac.

You've never been well-off, have you? Was there ever a period in your life when you didn't have to count your money before payday?

No, there's never been a time when we didn't have to count our money. I don't know. Probably you'd have to own a large business in order to not count your money.

Are you the one who runs the family finances?
Yes.

Vladimir Putin:

Lyuda is still basically running the finances. I didn't use to pay attention to our family finances, and I won't start now. I'm not very good at saving money. And what should I save it for? I believe that you need to have a comfortable living space, eat normally, dress decently, provide your children with a good education, and go away somewhere on vacation every once in awhile. That's all you need money for. What else would you need it for?

If I had a pile of money, I would travel. I would take a journey. I haven't been to many exotic countries. I've only been to America twice—to New York, in the sweltering heat, and also to Los Angeles. You don't see much when you're traveling on business—the airport, the hotel, the conference room, the airport. That's it.

I'd like to go on safari in Africa. To Kenya. I wanted to take my children there, but they were afraid of all the necessary shots. I'd like to travel to India. I've never been to any Arab countries. I'd like to see Egypt and Saudi Arabia. I've never been to Latin America at all. That would be interesting, too. They say that it looks like the Soviet Union in the 1950s.

Do you do the cooking at home?
I used to cook breakfast, lunch, and dinner. Now we have a cook.

Have you ever noticed that when somebody takes up a serious post in our country, they begin to gain weight?

Volodya works out every morning for 20 to 30 minutes. And he swims in the morning and the evening.

Vladimir Putin:

I usually don't have lunch. I don't have time. In the morning, I try to eat fruits and drink some kefir when I can. And when I don't manage to, I'd prefer not to eat anything at all. I eat in the evening. I'm not on a diet, but I also don't want to gain weight. Lyudmila has lost 15 kilograms, and I didn't even expect it. My girls are very slender as well.

At the prime minister's dacha, where we are now living, there's a little pool—about 12 meters long. I try to swim every day. And experience has shown it is better not to give up my workouts. If I give them up, I immediately have to buy clothes several sizes larger. I had a period, as I was saying, when I went from a size 44–46 to a 52. Then I took myself in hand. So at home I try to work out at least half an hour a day.

I have to tell you, it has reached the point of insanity. I told everyone that I used to do martial arts, and now people call me and say, "We have a tournament scheduled. When should it be held?" "What?" I ask. And they repeat, "We have a tournament scheduled, but when do you think we should have it?" And I say, "Have it whenever you like." And they ask, "When is it convenient for you? You'll be coming, won't you?" Well, I can't contain myself and I tell them to go to hell: "If I can come, I will, and if I can't, I won't. Don't be ridiculous!"

You went skiing together near Sochi, in Krasnaya Polyana. Did you get addicted to skiing in Germany?

No, before. The children ski better than we do. But they had guests that day and didn't go with us.

Vladimir Putin:

I've been skiing for a long time. I used to go to Cheget, and to Slavsk, in Ukraine. I've been abroad a few times. Lyudmila skis as well. Last time we went she was pretty good. People were amazed to see us in Sochi in February. But their reaction was very kind and human. Maybe because we didn't have 150 bureaucrats with us who didn't know how to ski but were waiting to hold the ski poles.

We went down the first time, and then I went over to the lift and took my goggles off. A line had formed, and suddenly I heard shouts of "It can't be!" People began letting us through to the head of the line. Nobody bothered us, really. Some wanted to take photographs. A group of people gathered around us, and we were photographed all together. I did refuse to give autographs, because I was there to ski and I would have gotten stuck signing autographs the whole time. It was funny. Somebody said, "How can it be that you're here among us, skiing?!" I laughed. "But who should I ski among? The Africans? They don't know how to ski—they don't have any snow."

Do you wait for your husband to get home in the evening?

Yes. And I get up with him in the morning. You know, before he became prime minister, it was easy to get up in the morning, even though we went to bed at midnight or 1 A.M. We were less tired. Now, it's a huge load. It seems just inhuman to me. I was horrified when I saw his meeting with Madeleine Albright on TV. He had slept about four hours the night before, and he had a three-hour meeting with Albright—and it wasn't just a social visit.

Aren't you amazed at the way he manages all of this?

I am amazed. Of course, Volodya always had a good memory. I remember when he was still working in Peter. We were invited to a reception at the French consulate. This was at the very start of his career. Volodya was late, and all of us—about seven people—were waiting for him. When he arrived, people threw questions at him, and for two hours he practically gave a press conference, even though we had just been invited for a visit.

What did he talk about?
Oh, everything. It was the first time I saw him in action. I sat there openmouthed. He talked about politics, the economy, history, and the law. I listened, and I kept thinking, "How does he know all this?" But you know, I always somehow believed in him. He had to start from zero so many times, and it always worked out. And in Moscow it all came together. You know, he had a hard time after he left the post of vice mayor. He couldn't find work. That period was really difficult for him. He was silent. He didn't say anything, but I understood. I still believe in him, although I'm a little afraid for him.

Your husband's status has changed dramatically, and that must affect your life. Strange as it seems, you must suffer from more limitations. Your friends can't just up and visit you. Your girls are growing up, isolated from friends . . .
And they are kept home from school, too, because the security measures have increased. Masha is in ninth grade, and Katya is in eighth grade. The teachers come to our home. But girlfriends come over as well. They still go to the movies, to the theater. . . . Of course, they're less free than they were before. But our girls have turned out to be—knock wood—somehow very smart about life. I hope all these changes don't affect them.

Masha:

To be honest, I'd like to go to school. Of course, they ask all sorts of questions about Papa there. Polite people don't ask, but rude ones do. The ones who are really curious. When Papa became prime minister, people began to treat us with a lot more respect, it was really noticeable. But you know, some of them would flatter us or try to get in good with us. And that really bothers me. Some of them would be telling others on the street, "I know that Putin girl." But on the whole, the friends I had last year are still my friends.

Katya:

We're not really concerned about politics. We ask Papa to watch cartoons and sometimes he joins us. Our favorite movie right now is *The Matrix*, but Papa hasn't seen it. We invited him to see it with us. He said he didn't have time now, but he would definitely see it later. First we went to the movie theater on Krasnaya Presnya Street and watched the film with Russian subtitles. Then we bought the cassette in English. We have three languages in school— German, English, and French.

Masha:

They give us a lot of homework. Even if we don't go to school, we still have a lot of homework. . . .

Katya:

We have guards when we go to the movies. There's a guy who sits there watching the movie, but I think he's guarding us at the same time. Usually, we don't even notice the bodyguards. Even when we go somewhere with our friends, they stay nearby, but they try not to get in the way. We've called them over to drink coffee with us a thousand times, but they don't want to.

Masha:

Sometimes people ask us, "Do you know what your Papa intends to do?" We never ask him. Why would we? He's already getting asked a bunch of questions. We spend more time telling him about ourselves. I think it's more interesting to him.

It seems like the two of them get along. Wasn't it hard to have them one after the other like that?

Volodya wanted it that way. He really loves the girls a lot. Not all men treat their girls as lovingly as he does. And he spoils them. I'm the one who has to discipline them.

He didn't want a boy?

He always said, "Whatever God gives us is good." He never said he wanted a boy.

Now, that white, fluffy thing over by the door—is that a girl or a boy?

She's a girl, too. Her name is Toska. She's a toy poodle. She hasn't had her hair cut in a long time. Volodya was sort of amazed by her at first—she's so little—but now he loves her.

Do Masha and Katya talk about the future? What would they like to be when they grow up?

Masha pronounces the English word *management* very seriously; and Katya says that she'd like to be a furniture designer.

The girls probably never see their father.

They see him more often on television than at home. But he always goes in to see them, no matter what time he gets home. We have a rule with Masha and Katya that they must be in bed by 11 P.M. If they go to bed later, then they can't have anyone over on Saturdays. It's probably too strict, but otherwise they'll stay up until 3 A.M. I'm all for self-discipline: You can stay up until 3, but you know what the consequences are.

And they can probably wrap Papa around their little fingers?
Nobody can wrap Papa around their little finger.

What's that book in German? Do you read German?
Yes, our daughters' teacher gave us this. She's German. It's a very interesting present, very touching. I haven't read it yet.

Vladimir Putin:
You know what the book is called? My wife translated it as "Talented Women in the Shadow of Their Great Husbands." But that's not completely accurate. The literal translation is "Gifted Women in the Shadow of Their Famous Husbands." I think that sounds much less complimentary to the husbands. The women are gifted, and the men are just famous.

Women who are in the shadow of their politician husbands probably have a complicated life. Women want attention. They like to be coddled . . .
I don't need to be coddled. I'm more like the women in those old Russian tales—"She stops a horse in mid-gallop, and runs into a burning hut." These are women who don't need coddling.

But everybody's interested in the wives of famous politicians. Have you never gotten mad at the press?
"Mad?"—that isn't quite the right expression. You get mad at people who are close to you, who matter to you. Of

course, there have been some unpleasant episodes. It's unpleasant, for example, when a journalist bothers your mama and your sister for interviews—without any warning, taking advantage of their naïveté. It's unpleasant when they dig into your background. It's unpleasant when they lie.

What is your husband's attitude toward the press? Does he watch TV?
The news and sometimes a movie.

Does he react at all?
Either he laughs or he gets upset, or he worries. I would say he reacts quite emotionally. On Saturday or Sunday, if we're home, he watches the analytical programs.

Vladimir Putin:
I read all the newspapers. The actual newspapers, not digests. It doesn't matter what order I read them in. I just start with whatever's on top. I read *Izvestia, Komsomolskaya Pravda, Sovetskaya Rossiya, Kommersant.* I watch the news if there's time. I've watched *Kukly,** but only a couple of times; it doesn't annoy me, but my friends take offense. Friends no doubt have the right to do that.

Do you have friends?
I have three girlfriends.

And your husband?
It always seemed to me that half of St. Petersburg was friends with Volodya. We always had a full house. Especially on weekends, but even during the week. Somebody was always coming over—usually at Volodya's invitation. He

*Kukly *is a satirical puppet show.*

loves socializing with people. I think that if he didn't, he wouldn't have been able to handle the stress. His friends from Peter come to visit us here and stay overnight.

Vladimir Putin:

The lack of contact with friends has really weighed on me, because I have some very good friends. In fact, our friends are our lives, they are us, they are a part of ourselves. I felt this keenly when I went to work abroad. The first few years, I missed my friends terribly. Without them, it was all empty and lonely. Although I had a heavy workload at my job, and a family and a home, I realized that our identity is in our friends. After our third year in Germany, we began to adapt and develop new ties. And suddenly I realized that I wasn't looking forward to going home on holiday. Really! It startled me.

I have a lot of friends, but only a few people are really close to me. They have never gone away. They have never betrayed me, and I haven't betrayed them, either. In my view, that is what counts most. I don't even know why you would betray your friends. For your career? Career alone doesn't mean much to me. Of course, a career offers you the opportunity to make something of yourself, to do something interesting. But how can you make something of yourself if you are betraying yourself? It's all very simple. If you look at a career as a means to achieve power, control people, or make money, and if you are prepared to lose everything doing that—well, that's another matter. But if you have priorities in life—benchmarks and values—then you realize that there's no point in sacrificing yourself and those who are a part of your life. There just isn't any point. You lose more than you gain. That's the way it is.

You probably have to go to receptions, be visible, and observe etiquette. Is your husband's social life a burden?

Not if there's somebody to chat with. And it's fun to dress up. Women like to dress nicely. On the other hand, politics itself has never interested me. It's boring.

Would you rather wear a skirt or pants?

Now I prefer skirts, but before it was pants. For everyday life I love knits—a skirt and sweater. But for official meetings now I have to wear suits.

In the old days, the wives of the leaders used to buy clothes in a closed section of GUM.* Now where do you go shopping?

In the same stores as everybody else. I recently went to Escada and bought the pants and the sweater I'm wearing right now. I spent a week driving around town looking for some boots for myself. I never found them. I couldn't find the right size.

Do you buy your husband's clothes?

There was a time when I shopped for him. And I still do, now and then. Clothes have never meant much to him. He's always had two—or, at the most, three—suits. And then jeans and shirts. At home he usually wears jeans and a sweater. He dresses very casually. But now, because he's always in the public eye, he has begun to dress a little more carefully.

Many people noticed that the sleeves of his suits used to be too long. Now they're okay.

That was my fault. Sometimes I was just too lazy to shorten his sleeves. Now he goes to a tailor.

If you buy him a tie, does he wear it without complaining?

Only if it goes with his shirt and suit. And no, he doesn't do anything without complaining.

---

*GUM is a Moscow department store.

You used to have long hair, and now you wear it short. Where do you get your hair done?

At Irina Baranova's. She used to do Nina Iosifovna Yeltsina's hair too. I think Irina is wonderful. She has her own salon.

And who's your husband's barber?

There are various barbers, either at the FSO or the FSB.* He's never paid much attention to his haircut. I like it when his hair is cut very short.

Do you go on vacation together?

We used to. Twice we went to Kurskiy Zaliv [Courland Lagoon] in Latvia. We've been abroad. But now . . . you know, I don't make plans anymore. I used to make them, and when they fell apart I would get very upset and offended. But now I understand it's easier not to make plans for shared vacations or holidays or time off, so as not to be disappointed.

You sound so sad when you say that.

No, not at all. I knew it would be like this. After all, if I was only worried about myself, then at some point I would have said to my husband, "Volodya, I beg you, don't do that. Let's stay on the sidelines. Let's do something else." But I didn't say that.

---

*The FSO is the Federal Guard Service (the personal protection corps of the president and other high officials), while the FSB is the Federal Security Service (the KGB's successor, working on domestic and foreign intelligence).

Part 9

THE POLITICIAN

Putin tackles the toughest issues in Russia today—the brutal war in Chechnya, the conflict in Kosovo, squabbles with NATO, financial scandals, corruption, and the weakness of the Russian judicial system. He discusses people—Yeltsin, Clinton, the people he trusts, the people he doesn't—and recreates the moment Yeltsin offered him the reins of power. Was he ready to govern one of the most complex, formidable, and volatile countries in the world? Would he ever be?

Your wife told us that you once gave an impromptu press conference to the French and spent two hours answering tricky political questions. Would you risk doing the same thing with us?

What are we going to talk about?

Everything.

What you're trying to achieve in Chechnya is more or less clear: a final ousting of the rebels. Do you know what to do in Chechnya after that?

First, we have to finish the military operation. What does that mean? We have to break up the major bandit formations—that is, units of ten or more fighters. Simultaneously we need to strengthen the role of law enforcement agencies and restore government agencies. We have to tackle social problems, schools, and hospitals. We must more actively create jobs. Then hold elections.

We need to hold a by-election for a parliamentary representative from Chechnya. The republic must have its own deputy in the Russian Duma. Depending on how the situation turns out, the introduction of direct presidential rule may be necessary.

Direct presidential rule? For how long?

For a year or two. During that time, we have to restore all the governmental agencies and transition to other new political procedures: that is, elections to the local governing bodies, and to the post of leader of the republic. And as a necessary precondition, to form a base of reliable people.

Will you appoint them from Moscow? Will they be Russians or Chechens?

Various options are possible, including a mixed leadership. There are many possibilities. That's something we will have to decide. We have to choose people not by their ethnic characteristics but by their abilities.

But we've already had all that, although in a different form— elections, and the government agencies, and the social assistance. And then the rebels took Grozny back in a heartbeat. There's no guarantee this won't happen again.

You know what the guarantee is? I repeat: The bandits will be destroyed. Whoever takes up arms will be destroyed. And we're prepared to do business with all the rest. Let them elect a head of the republic. We are prepared to sign an agreement with Chechnya. How many power limitation agreements are there? Humans have developed an enormous number of ways to help different people in one state live in harmony. Yes, some sort of compromise has to be sought, and we will seek it. But no one will force any sort of decision on us.

But aren't we forcing it on them? Do you really think that no one will seek revenge? Not one person?

Russia was provoked into taking action. After all, the bandits are robbing Chechnya, robbing their own people. For three years, they have been stealing people's pay, pensions, and aid. And the majority of Chechens believe that their rulers are to blame.

But you're intending to establish *diktat*.

Nothing of the kind. We are using force against the bandits, not the people. The bandits are the ones who are trying to dictate to Chechens how they should live and even how they should pray to Allah. We will establish order. There will be peace and quiet in the republic. And then we'll move on to elections, and we'll make an agreement with the new leadership about the power relationship between Chechnya and the federal center, understanding that we still have to live together.

Do you have any better suggestions? Should we leave again, drop everything, and then wait for them to attack us? Isn't that a crime? Wouldn't it be a crime to abandon ordinary Chechens and to undermine Russia?

Or stay in Chechnya and wait to be attacked? What should we do?

I have said what we must do. We must go through the mountain caves and scatter and destroy all those who are armed. Perhaps after the presidential elections, we should introduce direct presidential rule there for a couple of years. We must rebuild the economy and the social services, show the people that normal life is possible. We must pull the young generation out of the environment of violence in which it is living. We must put a program of education in place . . . We must work. We must not abandon Chechnya as we did before. In fact, we did a criminal thing back then, when we abandoned the Chechen people and undermined Russia. Now we must work hard, and then transfer to full fledged political procedures, allowing them and us to decide how we can coexist. It is unavoidable fact: We must live together.

We have no plans to deport Chechens, as Stalin once solved the problem. And Russia has no other choice. Nobody can impose a solution on us by force but we are prepared to take maximum consideration of Chechen interests. We will negotiate and search for a compromise for our coexistence. And when they come to realize that this is an acceptable solution, they won't want to take up arms anymore.

But until they come to realize this, peaceful residents will turn into bandits and attack liberated settlements, and it's not clear whether they will ever understand this. We will destroy those who resort to arms. And we will have to create a local elite, which understands that it is in Chechnya's interests to remain part of Russia. As things stand today, any discussion of any status outside of the framework of Russia is out of the question.

The rebels have already sentenced you to death several times.

One should never fear such threats. It's like with a dog, you know. A dog senses when somebody is afraid of it, and bites. The same applies here. If you become jittery, they will think that they are stronger. Only one thing works in such circumstances—to go on the offensive. You must hit first, and hit so hard that your opponent will not rise to his feet.

The army will do its business and then go back into its barracks.

Chechnya isn't the whole country. What do you think the country needs above all? What's the main priority?

We must clearly and accurately determine our goals—not just speak about them in passing. These goals must become comprehensible and accessible to every person. Like the Code of the Builder of Communism.

And what would you write in the first line of this Code?

Moral values.

Will we once again search for Russia's special path?

You don't have to search for anything, it's already been found. It's the path of democratic development. Of course, Russia is a very diverse country, but we are part of Western European culture. No matter where our people live, in the Far East or in the south, we are Europeans.

All that remains is for Europe to think that, too.

We will fight to keep our geographical and spiritual position. And if they push us away, then we'll be forced to find allies and reinforce ourselves. What else can we do?

Bring Babitsky back!*

I think you have to direct that request to the bandits.

Andrei Babitsky is a Russian journalist who works for the U.S.-funded Radio Liberty and has written highly graphic accounts of the horrors of the war in Chechnya from behind rebel lines. Frustrated by his "unpatriotic" journalism and his coverage of Russian atrocities, the Russian government arrested him in February 2000 and then handed him over to the Chechen rebels, allegedly in exchange for several Russian POWs. Babitsky himself then reported that in fact he had been handed over to pro-Moscow Chechens working for the Russian army. This conversation took place before Babitsky's release in March 2000 under pledge not to leave Moscow pending investigation.

But people doubt that he is really being held by the rebels.
Really? Well, they shouldn't. And Cochetel?* Where is he?
And where is General Shpigun?** And they are holding 258
people. Where are they?

Cochetel didn't even manage to photograph anything. He
came across the Georgian border and he was seized immediately. Now he is sitting in a basement and writing letters: "I
can't endure it any longer. Do anything to set me free." And
Maskhadov*** has been saying up until now that he has no
idea where the Frenchman is, but he recently called Lord Russell-Johnston**** and offered to swap him.

So it turns out that Maskhadov does after all, control the
situation. He just won't admit it. Which means that he can't
be trusted. So when he says he knows nothing about Babitsky's whereabouts and that he doesn't know the field com-
manders who were interceding on his behalf, we obviously
can't believe him.

*Vincent Cochetel is an official from the U.N. High Commissioner for Refugees who
was kidnapped and released in 1998 before this interview. Putin may be confusing
him with Brice Fleutiaux, a French freelance photojournalist who was kidnapped in
October 1999 while working in Chechnya and was still being held hostage by
Chechen rebels as of March 2000.

**On March 5, 1999, unidentified persons abducted General Gennady Shpigun at
gunpoint at the airport outside Chechnya's capital. General Shpigun, a native of
the Caucasus, was the representative in Chechnya of the Russian Interior Ministry
and was still being held hostage as of March 2000.

***Aslan Maskhadov is the President of Chechnya, elected in democratic elections
in 1996.

****Lord Russell-Johnston was elected president of the Parliamentary Assembly of
the Council of Europe in January 1999.

Is Babitsky alive?

Yes, he is alive. I think the rebels even sent a video today. You can see very clearly in the video that he is alive.

When will he show up in Moscow?

He'll show up. And as soon as he shows up, he will be summoned for interrogation.

That's odd. First you release him against a written pledge not to leave Moscow, then you exchange him, and then you summon him for interrogation.

I'll tell you this: Our country is going through a rather complex period of time. You would agree that Russia's defeat in the first Chechen war was due to a large extent due to the state of society's morale. Russians didn't understand what ideals our soldiers were fighting for. Those soldiers gave their lives and in return they were anathematized. They were dying for the interests of their country and they were publicly humiliated.

This time around, fortunately, it's different. Babitsky and his ilk were essentially trying to reverse the situation. He was working directly for the enemy. He was not a neutral source of information. He was working for the bandits.

So you don't like his reports?

Can I please finish? He was working for the bandits. So, when the militants said they were ready to release several of our soldiers in exchange for him, our people asked him, "Do you want to be exchanged?" And he said, "Yes."

And in exchange we were offered three of our soldiers who were under death threats if we didn't rescue them. These were our soldiers. They were fighting for Russia. If we didn't get them back, they would be shot. But the bandits wouldn't do anything to Babitsky because they thought of him as one of their own.

And then they told us: if you give us back Babitsky, then as soon as he gets to our camp in the mountains, we'll let go another two POWs. And they did release them. So, in sum, it was one of Babitsky versus five of our soldiers. It would have been worth exchanging him for just one Russian soldier.

So now he's a hero of Russia?

Or a traitor? It's not good to collaborate with bandits and to write that they are cutting off the heads of our soldiers in order to portray the whole horror of war. And the fact that they were cutting off peoples' heads alive before the start of hostilities, and the fact that they took the hundred hostages for criminal motives in order to get ransom—how do you account for that? Babitsky was justifying the decapitation of people.

What he said exactly was . . .

I have read it. He went there. He went in. And he came out carrying maps of routes that showed how to skirt around our checkpoints. What authority did he have to stick his nose in there without official accreditation?

Then perhaps he should have been brought to Moscow to sort the whole matter out here?

He was arrested and an investigation was started. He said: "I don't trust you. I trust the Chechens. They asked that I be handed over to them, so hand me over." And our people said to him, "The hell with you."

And what if it is all untrue?
You may ask me some other time to tell you the truth about the war. What really happens to people when they fight on the side of the enemy . . .

Journalists don't fight.
What Babitsky did is much more dangerous than firing a machine gun.

And what about freedom of expression?
We interpret freedom of expression in different ways. If you mean direct complicity in crimes, I will never agree with that. Let us repeat the sentence about decapitation.

Please, you can speak your mind, but you have no right to determine his fate.
We didn't stick him in there. He went himself.

Are you sure?
That's the truth. What I say is confirmed by his own words and what you say isn't confirmed by anything.

And the tape, where you can see quite clearly just how much he wants to go there . . . * They took a Russian journalist and gave him to God knows who.
He's not a Russian journalist.

He's a Russian citizen.

---

*In a videotape of Babitsky delivered to Radio Liberty after he was said to be turned over to Chechen rebels, he looked pale and tired, spoke slowly, and said he wanted to go home.

Well, you say he's a Russian citizen. Then let him behave according to the laws of his own country, if he wants those same laws to be applied to him.

Still, it isn't clear, under what law could you hand him over?
He asked for it himself.

And if he had asked for you to execute him, would you?
That's impossible. That is prohibited by the internal regulations. I'll tell you this. It's senseless to execute him, but getting five of our soldiers for him—I think that's quite acceptable.

Bring back Babitsky.
We can't bring him back. We will hunt for him and turn him over to the courts. I don't know if this case has any prospect of coming to trial. I'm not certain about that. But he'll have to be interrogated.

What's wrong with our relationship with NATO?
We don't feel like we're full-fledged participants in the process. If we were granted full-fledged participation in decision-making, then things wouldn't be so terrible.

The situation with Yugoslavia illustrates that decisions can be made without Russia.
That's just the point! We don't need those kinds of relations.

You were secretary of the Security Council, when the events in Yugoslavia began. Was the president or the prime minister interested in your opinion?

The president decided these matters directly with the Ministry of Defense and the Foreign Ministry.

But if you had been in Primakov's place, would you have turned the plane around over the Atlantic?*
Possibly. Primakov was in a very difficult position. Yes, he could have flown to Washington and used his visit as a tribunal to express Russia's position. But the Americans could have turned such a visit around for their own purposes. They could have interpreted the arrival of the Russian prime minister as a sign that Russia agreed with their proposed option for resolving the Yugoslav problem.

Their means of resolving the problem in Yugoslavia was predetermined after the fall of the USSR.

Then why these demonstrations, if a weakened Russia could not do anything?
That's not true. Even in its current state, there's a lot that Russia can do. We should have analyzed the situation earlier—before the bombing of Yugoslavia—to see how we could have influence our partners' decision. We could have worked more actively with the countries that did not agree with the turn of events.

Since we're talking about cooperation with Europe, let's return to Chechnya for a minute. Can you imagine allowing a peacekeeping force into Chechnya?
That's out of the question. If we were to recognize that Chechnya is an independent state, then yes, it would be pos-

In March 1999, then Prime Minister Yevgeny Primakov was on his way to the United States to discuss the Balkans crisis with President Clinton. When he learned that the Americans had made the decision to bomb Serbia, he turned the plane around and returned to Russia.

sible. Then Chechnya could decide to bring any peacekeeping forces it wanted.

They said that Kosovo would remain within Yugoslavia, and yet they brought in the troops.

That's why we are not agreeing to any options like Kosovo. Nothing analogous to the Kosovo events is possible. And it will never be possible. Everything that the NATO allies actually achieved in Kosovo directly contradicted the goals that NATO had established for itself.

You say, "We are not agreeing." Have they really made such offers?

Let's say that we are being offered mediators to help resolve the Chechen conflict. We don't need any mediators. That is the first step toward internationalizing the conflict— first come the mediators, then someone else, then observers, then military observers, and then a limited contingent of troops. And away we go. . . .

But what about OSCE observers?

In Chechnya? After military operations are completed and the bandit formations are totally defeated. They will be allowed in when we tell them, and where we consider it expedient.

With that kind of approach, it looks like integration into Europe isn't on the horizon.

It depends on what kind of Europe you mean. Let's analyze it: Yes, the world has changed, and Europe, too, has changed—that's no secret. The UN Charter was signed with a different array of world powers in mind. We were the main victors after World War II.

But now, alas, we have become weaker, and the UN Charter remains in effect. Not everybody likes that. They are trying to change it or supplant it—for example, with decisions from NATO. We must not agree to that.

Many have forgotten, by the way, that when NATO was created at the end of the 1940s, the Soviet Union indicated its intention to enter this bloc. But we weren't let in. In response, together with the countries of Eastern Europe, we formed the Warsaw Pact, which no longer exists. The Pact was a direct response to the formation of the NATO alliance.

So should we reconsider joining NATO?

We can consider it, but not at this moment. It's a question of *what kind* of NATO we're talking about. If we're talking about the NATO that acted in Kosovo in direct violation of UN decisions, that's not even of theoretical interest for us to discuss. If we're talking about a serious transformation of this bloc into a political organization prepared to have constructive interactions with Russia, then there is a topic for discussion.

In sum, I don't see any reason why cooperation between Russia and NATO shouldn't develop further; but I repeat that it will happen only if Russia is treated as an equal partner.

In any case, even when you are making suppositions, you have to think of the long term. There are a lot of problems— political, economic, military. For example, any bloc—and NATO is no exception—sets weapons standards that substantially affect the interests of the defense industry.

But what do the members of NATO think about this?

I think they fear the destruction of NATO from within. I understand them perfectly well. We are too powerful a dominant theme. There is one single power—the USA. Say a second one appears, albeit one not as powerful as the first. Yet the balance of power could be ruined. The founding fathers of NATO fear that their organization would change drastically. From our perspective, it would change for the better, and from theirs, possibly for the worse.

Still, it doesn't make sense. It seems as though Russia criticized NATO because we weren't allowed into the Yugoslavia resolution process as full-fledged partners. But what if we had been allowed in?

Well, that's just the point. If we had been allowed in, that decision never would have been made. We never would have agreed to that type of interference in the internal affairs of another country. That sort of behavior simply cannot be justified, even for so-called humanitarian reasons. I believe that the operation itself was a major mistake in international relations and a violation of the founding principles of international law.

And the invasion of Hungary by Warsaw Pact troops in 1956, and of Czechoslovakia in 1968? Were they major mistakes?

You forget that we used force in Germany in 1953, too. In my view, these were major mistakes. And the Russophobia that we see in Eastern Europe today is the fruit of those mistakes.

But look: We began talking about Russia's relationship with Europe, and we have narrowed it down to our relations with NATO. Even with the North Atlantic orientation of today's European policy, we cannot forget that NATO and Europe are not one and the same thing. And I've already said that Russia is a country of European culture—not NATO culture.

We're always hearing that Russia has grown weak, and that a whole slew of problems are ensuing from that weakness, both at home and abroad. Your thesis is that Russia's statehood must be restored—a strong state is needed. That's understandable. Does that mean that state property also has to be restored?

No, of course not. But we have to have state property on a limited scale, where it is necessary. For example, in the defense industry.

Does that mean that the private sector should be expanded?

First, we need to guarantee property rights. I believe that one of the main purposes of the state is to create rules—universal rules—in the form of laws, instructions, and regulations. And secondly, to comply with these rules, and guarantee their compliance.

But we've already had lots of these instructions and rules, regulations, and laws, and where have they gotten us?

You're right. And that is why the people do not trust the government. Look at all the types of laws that have been passed in the social sphere—for example, free transportation for members of the military. They may have passed the law, but in reality, the military pays for transportation. There are lots of other examples. In order to change this situation, the government will have to take some unpopular measures.

What unpopular measures?

We will have to review all the social guarantees that the state has taken upon itself in recent years and that are completely unfounded and not backed up. We have no choice.

Can you be more specific? Maybe you could use the example of free rides for military personnel?

Sure. Wouldn't it be better to raise the salaries of some citizens, including military people? If you gave them just a little bit more money, they could pay their own fares and wouldn't be put in such a humiliating position. But if the government does say that it will compensate those citizens—for example, for their fares—then it must do so.

I'm sure the leftist opposition will jump on me, saying that people are losing their benefits and that this is a blow against the helpless working people, who already have it so hard. But a government that doesn't fulfill its obligations is not a government. And that's why there's such a lack of trust in the government now.

So you are entering into a deal with the leftists because you'll need them when you have to make some unpopular decisions? Is that why you needed Seleznev as speaker of the House?

I need them? On the contrary, I told both Seleznev and Zyuganov to find a fresh face, even if it's a person from their own camp.

But a Communist! You really wound up with a fresh face, didn't you! . . .

Listen, there has always been cooperation with the Communists in our Duma. Not a single law passes without support from the Communists. It seems to me that there is more than one way to deal with the Communists. They have every opportunity to become a modern parliamentary party in the European sense of the word. We have very many parties, groups, grouplets, and associations without any real social base. And then there are the Communists—the only large-scale, really big party with a strong social base, albeit one infested with ideological "roaches."

Name the "roaches" for us.
For example, the demands to confiscate and nationalize property.

That's not going to happen?
That's definitely not going to happen. We will not have another major tragedy. And we will not have a partnership with the Communists while they maintain that position. If some sort of unlawful actions in previous years were established and proven in court, that would be another matter. But nationalization and confiscation of property for their own sakes, without a judicial procedure is a catastrophe. If for no other reason than because they would clear the way for arbitrary rule.

Communists can either change their programmatic goals and become a major left-wing party of the European type, or they can take the other path and lose their social base through natural attrition. If they choose the latter, they will gradually exit the political stage.

They themselves hardly believe that.
As surprising as it may sound, their leaders do understand. And they are prepared to change their ways. But right now they can't do it—they're afraid that their constituency will feel betrayed. And on that score, it's pretty important not to miss the moment—when and to what extent they can change internally.

For many people, "strong authority" is associated with dictatorship.

I prefer another phrase—not "strong," but "effective" authority.

You can call it what you like. But how will that authority become effective? How will it enforce the rules it establishes?

The courts must work—as must the law enforcement agencies and the courts of arbitration. The role of these agencies has changed, and we refuse to understand that. Their role has begun to correspond to what is written in the law. Why don't we pay judges and law enforcement agents the money that they deserve? Because Soviet ideology governs our consciousness to this day. Remember how we used to think: "Well, a court, what's that? Nothing special. The district Party committee is the body that makes all the decisions. It's important. But what do the judges do? They will do what they are told."

To this day, people think that judges are not important, and that they shouldn't be paid more than the average civil servant.

Or take the notary publics. In the French system, if a notary public stamps a document, it is ironclad law. If a notary public makes a mistake, he is obliged to pay compensation. Two mistakes, and he is ruined.

Our society must understand that a minority—a certain category of people—must be paid very well by the state, so that they can secure the interests of the majority. When will we finally begin to understand this? Our people aren't stupid. It's just that it hasn't been explained the right way.

But the role of the courts has been explained. They've been explaining it for ten years! But until the courts change for the

better, the attitudes toward them won't change either. How else can you explain it?

More persistently. Without that, nothing will change. And we have to raise judges' salaries.

Now, the governors are hardly going to line up behind your ideas about "effective" authority and the governability of the state. They're all going to be afraid that you will cut off their independence.

I think that we have to preserve both local self-government and a system of election for governors. But all of these connections have to be more balanced. While preserving the system of electing governors, for instance, we should consider applying sanctions against them. To remove them from office, for example.

That is, elect some and remove others.

We can develop systems to link them more closely to the center. They cannot have complete independence.

Do you mean a system of oversight?

Oversight and influence. All members of the Russian Federation should be placed under equal economic conditions vís à vis the federal center. We have signed a huge number of agreements on the separation of powers, but some federation members have unjustified privileges that others don't.

Tatarstan, for example?

Tatarstan, for example.

Shaimiev* may not understand you.

**Shaimiev is the president of Tatarstan.*

You're wrong. He does understand. I recently discussed the problem with him in general terms. Shaimiev generally agreed with me.

Everyone understands what is eroding the overall economic and political sphere. And that is one of our priorities.

The next step is science and education. Without modern managers, without a contemporary understanding of what needs to be done, and without carriers of this understanding, it will be impossible to achieve results.

But those "carriers" have already left the country.

Not all of them. And we've preserved the most important thing—fundamental science and education. If we lose that, of course, it's the end.

Where are you going to get the money for all of this?

You know, we don't need that much money. The problem is not money. The problem is understanding.

Well what, for example, would you pay young specialists, taking into account their understanding?

Let's say they are offered about $5,000 a month in the West. What if we were to pay them, theoretically speaking, $2,000 a month?

Oy!

Yes. And I bet the majority would not leave the country under those terms. To live in your own country, surrounded by your own language and peopleclose to you—your friends, your relatives, your acquaintances—and receive a little more money than others for that—it's very advantageous.

Still, it doesn't make sense. You intend to pay higher salaries to judges, the state bureaucracy, and the army, and you will also need more money for education and science. Where are you going to get it? What if America decides tomorrow to sell its strategic oil reserves? The prices will fall, and then . . .

We have money, but it has been slipping through our fingers. Until there is a strong state, we will remain dependent on someone's strategic reserves.

You're a specialist in law. Is the law immutable?

The law has to be observed, but if it becomes outdated, it must be altered. One of the postulates of legal theory is that the law always lags behind life.

What about our Constitution? Is it lagging behind life?

The Constitution should enshrine the most general principles. Therefore it lives longer than ordinary law. This is natural, since the Constitution guarantees society certain rules for the long term. But amendments can be made to it.

Should amendments be made to the section in the Constitution about the powers of the president? Should they be limited? In fact, another type of amendment is being contemplated now—increasing the term of office of the president to seven years.

I don't know, maybe four years is enough time to get things done. But four years is a short term. The technical experts we're working with are mapping out a year-by-year program of action. During the first, the agenda is to form goals and teams; during the second and part of the third, to gradually achieve concrete results; during the end of the third and the beginning of the fourth, to present our results and to begin the next election campaign. If that cycle is broken and everything is scattered, we won't be able to get anything done, and we won't be able to prepare for the next elections.

What about the powers of the president?
I can't rule it out—amendments are possible. We must look carefully at how things are formulated and whether they correspond with the interests of the state and the society as a whole. If there are exceptional rights in the section on the powers of the president, then we should think about reviewing them. I believe this should be the subject of a broad discussion. But from the very beginning, Russia was created as a supercentralized state. That's practically laid down in its genetic code, its traditions, and the mentality of its people.

If you want to take a historical approach to these issues, then monarchy is also embedded in Russian tradition. Does that mean we should restore it?
I think that is not very likely. But in general . . . in certain periods of time . . . in a certain place . . . under certain conditions . . . monarchy has played and continues to this day to play a positive role. In Spain, for instance. I think the monarchy played a decisive role in releasing the country from despotism and totalitarianism. The monarchy was clearly the stabilizing factor. The monarch doesn't have to worry about whether or not he will be elected, or about petty political interests, or about how to influence the electorate. He can think about the destiny of the people and not become distracted with trivialities.

And the prime minister will think about everything else.
Yes, the government.

But in Russia, that's not possible.
You know, there's a lot that seems impossible and incredible and then—*bang!* Look what happened to the Soviet Union. Who could have imagined that it would simply collapse? No one saw that coming—even in their worst nightmares.

Were you present at the burial of the remains of the czar's family in St. Petersburg?
No.

What do you think? Was burying them the right thing to do?
I think so.

Should the state have relations with big business?
Definitely, because a lot depends on big business. But relations between the state and business should be defined by the law and by general rules. Businesses want this sort of regulation too, so that the state can't play favorites and so that they're all competing under equal conditions.

So you don't rule out dealing with big businessmen?
Of course not. I think the state has to listen to both workers and trade unions as well as to the representatives of big business and associations of entrepreneurs. Much depends on the policies of firms and major companies. How can I pretend that this doesn't matter to me? That would be a mistake. But the state should not command business.

On the question of favorites: in an interview, Boris Berezovsky* said that he meets with you once a month. Is that
true?

It's probably less often.

On whose initiative?

On his. He has such a lively mind. Most of his ideas are
connected to the Caucasus—to Chechnya and Karachay-
Cherkessia. He was, after all, deputy secretary of the Security
Council, and worked on these issues. Incidentally, in my view,
his proposals on Chechnya are not realistic or effective.
Frankly speaking, that is why nothing that he has proposed is
being implemented. From time to time, I not only meet with
Berezovsky but also with other businessmen—for example
Petr Aven, Potanin, and Alekperov.

**Your wife said that you don't like to discuss your work col-
leagues. But we're interested in people. In Boris Nikolayevich
Yeltsin, for example. . . .**

Do you want me to give you an evaluation of his role in
history?

**Well, you did have a relationship with him, including a per-
sonal one.**

I did not have a particularly close relationship with Boris
Nikolayevich, just a good working relationship. He treats me
very well and I am grateful to him for that. I hardly ever meet
him in regular life.

---

*Boris Berezovsky is a prominent and influential Russian businessman. He is part-
owner of ORT, a pro-government television station, and has taken an active role in
the Chechen conflicts. He was former deputy secretary of the National Security
Council in the Yeltsin administration.

And you don't play tennis?

And I don't play tennis. Before his retirement, I visited Yeltsin at home only on work-related matters. Moreover, I can say that only when he began to discuss the question of his resignation with me did I sense a certain warmth in him.

Do you call him?

Yes. He and I talk more now than we did before his retirement. Before, I wouldn't have dreamed of calling him. . . . That is, I did pick up the phone and call him a few times, but only for work matters. Now our relationship is different. Now I can just call him and chat.

But do you visit him?

Yes, I visit him. Recently I went to his house on business. Boris Nikolayevich said to me, "Please stay for dinner. We're going to have sushi." Apparently he once tried sushi in a restaurant and he liked it. So his wife and daughter decided to put together a Japanese meal at home. Of course I stayed. Afterward we sat for a long time drinking beer and talking.

Does Yeltsin call you himself?

Yes, he has called several times. He was intersted to find out how things were going in the Caucasus. And then he once asked how our internal troops were doing. He called about the CIS summit, and we met at his initiative to discuss how to raise certain issues during the meeting with the CIS leaders. And we discussed the leadership of the Commonwealth. His experience in this regard is very helpful.

Everyone is wondering whether you are going to lock horns with Luzhkov* like you did before?
Lock horns? But I never had any fight with him.

Alright, then. Will you try to break him, or will you work with him as with any other member of the Federation Council?**
Of course I'll work with him. I'm prepared to rely on him as someone with great influence in the largest region of the country—the capital—but his own actions must be directed at strengthening the state.

What were they directed at before?
Until now, to a large extent, they have been aimed at satisfying his political ambitions. When a regional leader is so ambitious, I think it is destructive for the country.

Actually, the fault lies not so much with the individual as with the central authority. As soon as the regional leaders sense that the government is strong and effective, they will return to the role prescribed for them by the Constitution, and begin to take care of business.

Like the Ring Road?
Yes, the Ring Road.

They say a lot of money was stolen on that project.
Whenever I hear someone accused of theft or something like that, I want to ask: Do we still presume people to be innocent? If a crime is not proven, no one can be accused of it.

---

*Yuri Luzhkov has been the mayor of Moscow since the Yeltsin era. Luzhkov was accused of embezzlement during his rebuilding of the Ring Road around Moscow.

**The upper chamber of Parliment, where the mayor of Moscow has a seat.

Of course, there is also a peculiarly Russian feature that is known to all. Remember that joke from the Soviet era? Brezhnev comes to visit Carter. Carter says, "Do you see that beautiful bridge there?" "Yes," says Brezhnev. Carter tells him: "It has five lanes running one way and five lines running in the opposite direction. But the plans called for 10 lanes one way and 10 lanes the other way." "Well, where are the missing lanes?" asks Brezhnev. "They're all here!" says Carter, and points to the furniture in the White House. Brezhnev thinks, "Well, alright!" Then Carter comes to visit him in Russia. Brezhnev says, "See the Moscow River?" "I see it," says Carter. "Do you see the bridge across it?" "No, I don't." "Because it's all right here!" says Brezhnev and he points to the furniture in the Kremlin.

Of course you can assume that somebody siphoned off funds from the construction of the Ring Road; but at least that road is out there, isn't it? And you can be proud of it. And if somebody thinks that somebody stole something, let him go and prove it.

How do you think Luzhkov is going to treat you?
I think he will behave constructively. I don't think he will really have a choice.

What are you implying?
Nothing. I'm not implying any forcible actions. You know, I think that many people believe that the president had ceased to be the center of power. Before, they behaved quite loyally. If need be, I will simply act in such a way as to guarantee that no one has such illusions anymore.

The most famous Petersburger is Anatoly Chubais. Do you have a close relationship with him? Weren't you acquainted with him in Peter?

When I came to work for Sobchak, Chubais was the deputy chair of the Leningrad City Council executive committee. I never had any direct interaction with Chubais. I never dealt with him closely.

How did you react to his voucher plan?

I didn't.

What did you do with your own voucher?

I lost it, at first, and then I found it and bought something with it, something stupid. About a year before the privatization, I spoke with Vasily Leontiev, the Nobel Prize winner, and he told me, "Give the property away to whomever you wish. In two or three years it will end up in the right hands anyway. Give it away free if you have to." And Chubais did give it away. I think that was his exact approach—although, of course, you should ask him about it yourself.

Two or three years? Do you think that's inevitable?

I don't know whether it's inevitable. What's important is that the property be in the hands of an effective owner.

But it wound up in the hands of a different owner.

That's just it.

Weren't you offended when Chubais came to work in the presidential administration, and the first thing he did was eliminate the position that had been promised to you?

No, I wasn't offended. I know his technocratic approach to the solution of problems. He had decided that the existing staff structure did not correspond to the challenges that faced the administration.

There was nothing personal about it?

There is no question of intrigue here. He is not the sort of person who is guided by sentiments. Of course I can't say that I was overjoyed at the time, but I didn't feel angry at him. Quite frankly, I wasn't particularly hurt.

So when did you establish more or less regular contact with Chubais?

Never.

But he comes and visits you at your dacha on occasion?

Yes, he sometimes comes to visit.

Were you surprised that Chubais supported the operation in Chechnya?

Yes.

Why?

I thought that he lived in a world of illusions. But it turned out that he's more of a pragmatist, that he's capable of grasping the realities of life and is not guided by ephemeral ideas.

And when he said that he supported your candidacy in the presidential elections?

That didn't surprise me either, because he knows perfectly well that I am not a dictator and don't intend to return the country to an administrative economy ruled by directives.

Chubais, by the way, is a very good administrator. I've watched him run the Commission on Operations, and I've seen him in action at government meetings. He is able to grasp the main point, and as Vladimir Ilyich Lenin used to say, pull out the whole chain. But of course, he is so hard-nosed, like a Bolshevik ... yes, that's the right word to describe him. Unfortunately, he has a bad credit record. I mean his public credit—the public's trust in him—is low.

What political leaders do you find most interesting?
Napoleon Bonaparte. [Laughs.]

No, seriously.
De Gaulle, most likely. And I also like Erhard. He was a very pragmatic person. He was the one who built the new Germany after the war. In fact, his entire conception for the reconstruction of the country began with the creation of new moral values for society. For Germany, this was particularly important, after the collapse of Nazi ideology.

Why have you postponed all your trips abroad until after the elections?
It was a logistical problem: The president and the prime minister do not have the right to travel abroad at the same time, and I am simultaneously the acting president and the prime minister.

Any other reason? Were you afraid that you would be pecked apart over Chechnya?
I'd like to peck them all apart myself. But they didn't really want to meet with us because of Chechnya. Or if they were prepared to meet, it was in a format and at a level of discussion that did not suit us. They would meet with us on our terms, they said, if we agreed to change our position on the

Caucasus. That suited us even less, as it would have cost more than my trips abroad.

But when you were still a "traveling" prime minister, you managed to meet with Clinton in New Zealand.
Yes, I liked him.

What did you like about him?
He's a very charming person. I liked talking to him.

You evidently share a mutual admiration for each other. He recently supported you on the Internet.
In that first meeting, he also paid special attention to me. When we were in New Zealand—I don't recall whether it was at lunch or dinner—he made a point of coming up to me. We had been seated at different tables. We talked about something for a while, and then he said, "Well, shall we go?" Everyone lined up in a corridor—the leaders of other states, guests—and he and I walked together along that corridor. We exited the hall to the sound of applause. I appreciated this sign of special regard. Maybe that's why he made such a good impression on me. No, I'm just kidding around. In conversation, he just seems like a sincere person—open and friendly—and that's very important.

He has a natural charm.
Probably. If you don't have natural charm, it's very hard to learn it. I know that for sure.

Who else have you met personally?
Kohl, Thatcher, Major.

Was that back when you were working in Petersburg?
Yes.

Did you speak German with Kohl?
He met with Sobchak for about 30 minutes. I translated. They were the most general kind of remarks, about nothing really. We were at lunch. He had said, "Let's not talk about anything serious. Come to Bonn in about three weeks, and we'll talk about everything."

Later, Sobchak took him up on the offer, and took me along with him. It was a business trip. You know what surprised me the most? I didn't expect any major European political figure would know Russia so well and so deeply. That simply amazed me.

Now I can't recall everything that he said, but I do remember my own feelings. I was impressed by Kohl's deep knowledge of Russian history and contemporary life. He understood the essence of the events taking place. And it was especially gratifying to hear him say that he couldn't imagine a Europe without Russia. He said that the Germans were not only interested in the Russian market but in becoming worthy partners with Russia.

But maybe he was just using polite phrases.
No, I don't think so. These were not just the protocol phrases. I was convinced that he really felt what he said.

Such a strong leader, and such a scandal after his resignation! It's strange.
There's nothing strange about it. In fact, the Christian Democratic Union had grown weak and it was defeated.

Obviously, the leadership made mistakes. But after 16 years, any people—including the stable Germans—get tired of a leader, even a leader as strong as Kohl. It just took them a while to realize it.

Now you've arrived in the Kremlin, which in recent times has been linked to scandal after scandal of its own—Borodin and Mabetex,* the "Family" money**... You've been strangely silent about all this, and people are conjecturing that it's because the "Family" brought you in and that, in gratitude, you are putting out all the fires.

I never had any special relations with the people close to the president. And it would be very risky to trust such a serious matter as "putting out fires" to a little-known person.

It can't be that risky if you appointed Borodin to the post of state secretary for Belarus and Russia.
I didn't appoint him. I proposed him, and he was selected.

Even though he has a trail of scandalous accusations behind him? You don't believe that you should have investigated the scandals first, before nominating him for an official post?
I believe what is written in the law. There is a golden rule, the fundamental principle of any democratic system, and it is called "the presumption of innocence."

---

*Borodin was accused of providing kickbacks to Yeltsin and his family through the Swiss construction firm, Mabetex.

**The "Family" refers to Yeltsin, his family, and his entourage.

But nothing was proven in court in the case of Prosecutor General Yuri Skuratov,* and that didn't prevent him from being dismissed.

Skuratov was removed from his position in full compliance with the law, which states that during the period of investigation of a case opened against the prosecutor general, he must be removed. That's what happened.

Do you suppose that if the investigation doesn't find anything, he'll be reinstated?

Theoretically, yes. But there is more at stake here than just the criminal and legal aspects. There is a moral aspect as well. I am clear on the moral side of the story. I know the facts exactly. He and I spoke about this.

Then why did he later deny the story again?

Because he didn't want to be compromised, that's all.

A newspaper reported that Skuratov wrote his second letter of resignation after you worked him over. They also said that compared to you, the cellars of the FSB headquarters in Lubyanka seemed like paradise.

This is all nonsense.

But what happened?

The four of us met: Boris Nikolayevich, Prime Minister Primakov, myself, then director of the FSB, and Skuratov.

Boris Nikolayevich took out the videotape and the photographs made from the videotape. He just put them on the

---

A newspaper published photos purportedly showing Skuratov with prostitutes, which unleashed a scandal leading to his suspension as prosecutor general.

table and said, "I don't think that you should work as the prosecutor general any longer."

Primakov agreed: "Yes, Yuri Ilyich, I think that you had better write a letter of resignation." Yuri Ilyich thought for a while. Then he took out a piece of paper and wrote that he was resigning.

If you were in a similar situation, how would you have acted?

If I thought that my personal behavior was incompatible with my professional duties, of course I would leave. I am certain that the position of prosecutor general, for example, is incompatible with a scandal like this.

And the position of prime minister?

Prime minister? Strange as it may sound, it would be less serious. A prosecutor is different. A prosecutor should be a model of morality and scruples, because he is the one who ensures that all citizens comply with the law—the prime minister, the president, and everyone else.

Another question—this one, related to the heroines of this story. Should we fight prostitution?

Through social and economic means.

What kind?

We need for people to live normally. After World War II, prostitution flourished in Western Europe because people were poor. Talk to the veterans of World War II and they will tell you that women gave themselves away for a chunk of bread. Prostitution arises out of poverty and desperation. If you live a normal life, if the economy develops, if the standard of living rises. . .

In Germany there is already a high standard of living, and there's plenty of prostitution. It's even legalized.

But there are only foreign women in the brothels. There aren't any Germans.

How would you know?

So I've been told . . . by people like yourselves from the licentious professions.

Alright. So maybe there are no Germans, but there's prostitution.

There is prostitution. I'm talking now about the nationality of the participants. They're all operating openly. And there are no Germans among them, because the standard of living in the country is very high.

So are you for or against the legalization of prostitution?

I don't think that prostitution should be legalized. You have to combat it with social and economic methods. Then no one will want to go into prostitution. Why—are you in favor of legalization?

Well, you could have doctors in the brothels, then. And the girls would not be ripped off, or mistreated.

You have a kind heart.

Whose proposals do you listen to, and who do you trust? You said that your goal in the first year is to formulate a team. Who is on your team?

Trust? Sergei Ivanov, Secretary of the Security Council.

Have you known each other for a long time?

I've known him for a long time, but not very well. We began working together in the Leningrad Directorate of the KGB. At that time I only knew that he existed. Then he went to Moscow, and did several long stints abroad. We had many friends in common. I heard stuff about him from all different people, and it was positive. He knows several languages: English, Swedish, and Finnish, I think. And I think that he is in the right job. He recently returned from the States, where things went very well. He met with Clinton, Albright, and Berger. I'm happy with his work.

But there isn't anyone you've spent a lot of time with.

Of course, it is always better to have had the benefit of direct experience working together. But let's agree that there is such a thing as comradeship. I get that feeling with Ivanov and with Nikolai Patrushev and also with Dima Medvedev.

Medvedev is heading your election campaign. Is he also from Peter?

He taught civil law at Leningrad University. He has a doctoral degree in jurisprudence and is a fine expert. I needed some people when I worked with Sobchak in the mayor's office. I went to the law faculty for help, and they suggested Dima. When I was deputy mayor, Dima was my adviser, and he worked with me for about a year and a half. Then, after our unsuccessful elections, he left the mayor's office and went back to the university.

You recently invited him to Moscow?

Just this year. Actually, I had originally planned for Dima to head up the Federal Securities Commission. He is a specialist in the securities market. He seems to like to working on our team, but we haven't yet decided specifically where to use him.

Who else?

I trust Aleksei Kudrin. He is now first deputy minister of finances. I think that he's a decent and professional guy. We both worked for Sobchak and we were both his deputies. In years of working together, you can learn a lot about a person.

And where did Igor Sechin come from?

Sechin also worked with us in Petersburg, in the protocol department. He is a philologist by training. He knows Portuguese, French, and Spanish. He worked abroad, in Mozambique and Angola.

Was he in combat?

Yes. Then he landed on the executive committee of the Leningrad City Council. When I became deputy mayor and was choosing my staff, I considered a lot of people, and I liked Sechin. I suggested that he come to work for me. This was in 1992–1993. And when I went to work in Moscow, he asked to come along, so I brought him with me.

Now what will happen with the old guard in the Kremlin? Everyone says, just wait, Putin will win the elections and he'll be free of them. In the best case, he'll fire them.

You know, that kind of logic is characteristic of people with totalitarian mentalities. That's how they expect a person to behave if he wants to remain in his post the rest of his life. But I don't want that.

But there are some figures that the public has a uniformly negative reaction to, such as Pavel Borodin. Then there's also the chief of the presidential administration, Aleksandr Voloshin. He's not beloved by the public.

Voloshin is not well liked by the public, or by a part of the establishment. As groups and clans fought among themselves, a negative feeling emerged. Voloshin was not immune to it. And these clans fought dirty. I don't think that's a basis for firing someone. Voloshin suits me just fine for today. The work he is doing is rather particular. We discussed who could be put in his place, and we considered Dima Medvedev. Voloshin himself said, "Let Dima work as my deputy, and then, when he grows into the job, let him be considered as my replacement." There's no sense in second-guessing it now.

But it does make sense to respond to the public's criticism of officials in the Kremlin and the entourage of the former president.

I, too, have worked for the state for a long time. Am I in the entourage, or not? These questions are all about appearances. The individual, with his knowledge, his professional abilities, and his talents, is worth far more. I will be guided by whether a person fits the post he occupies or not. That's the most important thing.

In any event, I'm not president yet. First I have to win the elections. And to be honest, I'm a superstitious person, so I try not to think about these things ahead of time. Do you think I should?

You thought you might have to pay for this war with your career, but you became acting president instead.

It probably helped that I didn't want the president's job.

And when Yeltsin said that he planned to resign before the end of his term, you didn't say, "No, what are you doing, Boris Nikolayevich?!"

No, I didn't try to talk him out of it; but I also didn't dance with joy and thank him and assure him that I would justify his faith in me. My first reaction was "I'm not ready for this."

When I was appointed prime minister, it was interesting and it was an honor. I thought, "Well, I'll work for a year, and that's fine. If I can help save Russia from collapse, then I'll have something to be proud of." It was a while stage in my life. And then I'll move onto the next thing. About two or three weeks before New Year's Eve, Boris Nikolayevich invited me into his office and said that he had made the decision to resign. I would become the acting president. He looked at me and waited to see what I would say.

I sat in silence. He started to explain it in more detail—that he wanted to announce his resignation before New Year's ... When he stopped talking, I said, "You know, Boris Nikolayevich, to be honest, I don't know if I'm ready for this or whether I want it, because it's a rather difficult fate."

I wasn't sure I wanted such a fate. . . . And then he replied, "When I came here, I also had other plans. Life turned out this way. I, too, didn't strive for this, but in the end, circumstances forced me to fight for the post of president. Well, I think your fate is forcing you into a decision. Our country isn't so huge. You'll manage."

He paused and became lost in thought. I realized this was hard for him. On the whole, it was a depressing conversation. I had never thought seriously that I might become his successor, so when Boris Nikolayevich told me about his decision, I wasn't really prepared for it.

But I would have to respond one way or the other. The

question had been put to me: yes or no? When the conversation went off on a tangent for a while, I thought I was off the hook. I thought that it was all forgotten. But then Boris Nikolayevich looked me in the eye and said: "You haven't answered me."

On the one hand, there were my own internal arguments. But there was also another logic. My fate was allowing me to work at the highest level in the country and for the country. And it would be stupid to say, "No, I'd rather sell seeds" or "No, I'm going into private law practice." I could always do those things later. So I decided I would do it.

Katya:

I flipped out when I heard that Papa was going to become acting president. When Mama told me this, I thought she was joking. Then I realized that she wouldn't joke about such a thing. Then the phone kept ringing, and everyone was congratulating us. Our classmates, and even the school principal. She teaches us English. At midnight we turned on the TV and saw Papa shaking people's hands. I liked that. He was so serious . . . or calm. Really, just like always. Papa is Papa. On the one hand, I want him to become president. On the other, I don't.

Masha:

On the one hand, I don't want him to become president, and then on the other, I do want it. We also listened to Boris Nikolayevich speak that day. My throat started to hurt. Not like when you have a cold, but a different way. He really got to me.

Lyudmila Putina:

I learned about Boris Nikolayevich's resignation on the afternoon of the 31st. My girlfriend called me and said, "Have you heard?" I said, "What is it?" So I learned it from her. I cried for a whole day because I realized that our private life was over for at least three months, until the presidential elections, or perhaps for four years.

So, do you want to be president or not?

When I began to work as the acting president I felt . . . a satisfaction—perhaps that's not the best word—in making decisions independently, knowing that I was the last resort and that a lot depended on me. The responsibility was on me. Yes, I took pleasure in feeling responsible.

I have some rules of my own. One of them is never to regret anything. Over time, I came to the conclusion that this was the right thing to do. As soon as you start regretting and looking back, you start to sour. You always have to think about the future. You always have to look ahead. Of course you have to analyze your past mistakes, but only so that you can learn and correct the course of your life.

Do you like that kind of life?

You have to gain satisfaction from the process. We live each second, and we can never live that second all over again.

You say that so seriously, as if you've never committed any thoughtless stupidities, or wasted time on trivia.

I have done stupid things and wasted my time.

For example?

Okay. Once I was driving with my senior coach from Trud to a base outside Leningrad. I was in university at the time. A truck with a load of hay was coming from the other direction. My window was open, and the hay smelled delicious. As I drove past the truck on a curve, I reached out the window to grab some straw. The car suddenly swerved . . . Whoops! The steering wheel turned, and we were headed toward the rear wheel of the truck. I turned the wheel sharply in the other direction, and my rickety Zaporozhets went up on two wheels. I almost lost control of the car. We really should have ended up in a ditch, but fortunately, we landed back on all four wheels.

My coach sat there, frozen speechless. Not until we pulled up at the hotel and he got out of the car did he look at me and say, "You take risks." Then he walked away. There is some stupid stuff like that. What drew me to that truck? It must have been the sweet smell of the hay.

Vladimir Putin's "Russia at the Turn of the Millenium" is available on the PublicAffairs website at www.publicaffairsbooks.com. In this treatise, Putin analyzes the current challenges faced by Russia and proposes measures to improve Russia's future. The treatise first appeared on the website of the Government of the Russian Federation on December 31, 1999, while Putin was prime minister and acting president of Russia.

PublicAffairs is a new nonfiction publishing house and a tribute to the standards, values, and flair of three persons who have served as mentors to countless reporters, writers, editors, and book people of all kinds, including me.

I.F. STONE, proprietor of *I. F. Stone's Weekly*, combined a commitment to the First Amendment with entrepreneurial zeal and reporting skill and became one of the great independent journalists in American history. At the age of eighty, Izzy published *The Trial of Socrates,* which was a national bestseller. He wrote the book after he taught himself ancient Greek.

BENJAMIN C. BRADLEE was for nearly thirty years the charismatic editorial leader of *The Washington Post.* It was Ben who gave the *Post* the range and courage to pursue such historic issues as Watergate. He supported his reporters with a tenacity that made them fearless and it is no accident that so many became authors of influential, best-selling books.

ROBERT L. BERNSTEIN, the chief executive of Random House for more than a quarter century, guided one of the nation's premier publishing houses. Bob was personally responsible for many books of political dissent and argument that challenged tyranny around the globe. He is also the founder and longtime chair of Human Rights Watch, one of the most respected human rights organizations in the world.

For fifty years, the banner of Public Affairs Press was carried by its owner Morris B. Schnapper, who published Gandhi, Nasser, Toynbee, Truman and about 1,500 other authors. In 1983, Schnapper was described by *The Washington Post* as "a redoubtable gadfly." His legacy will endure in the books to come.

Peter Osnos, *Publisher*

Lightning Source UK Ltd.
Milton Keynes UK
UKOW05f0106030617

302598UK00004B/243/P